PIG FAT SOUP

SURVIVING MY USS PUEBLO PRISONER OF WAR JOURNEY

by Steven Woelk
As told to: Robert Lofthouse

Pig Fat Soup

Published by
Storyteller Publishing, LLC
1310 N. 78th Street
P.O. Box 9001
Kansas City, KS 66112

Table of Contents

Chapter 12

Introduction

The "USS Pueblo Incident" of 1968 is forever etched in the memories of the men who endured and survived the horrific story about the Pueblo. The North Koreans got their jollies intimidating, punishing, and beating these men for eleven months. Few people alive today are aware of this attack on the high seas. Fewer yet are aware of an incursion into South Korea by a North Korean commando unit which precipitated the whole international incident.

Sharing my experiences about Pueblo has never been challenging. That's somewhat surprising, because while each sailor and Marine endured his own measure of distress and humiliation, other than the death of Duane Hodges, I was the most severely wounded during the sea and air attacks on our ship.

This book gives a narrative of the whole traumatic tale and represents my unique perspective: an eye-witness account of a high-seas crime that resulted in my best friend's murder.

Multiple high-seas crimes have occurred over the years since the formal end of hostilities known as the Korean War, showing what the North Koreans are capable of:

> * **Piracy:** Forcibly boarding a ship, using violence or threats to take control.
>
> * **Human Trafficking:** Smuggling people across borders for exploitation.
>
> * **Violent Crimes:** Assaults, murders, and other violent acts.

North Korea is guilty of all three regarding their violent seizure of the Pueblo crew and ship.

A stunning recap by the Association for Diplomatic Studies and Training (ADST) reveals this story about two watershed moments in history. I've added my own personal eyewitness account of what took place. What did US government agencies and the Navy Department do and not do? Some of that will be highlighted in the story you are about to read.

As you learn about the Pueblo and her crew, the whole incident remains a symbol of embarrassment, incompetence, human resilience, prisoner of war defiance at the highest level, loyalty, homecoming, and a brotherhood that, for a moment in time, showed the steadfast courage of our crew, and how much the American people appreciated our faithfulness to duty.

This story captures what I saw and lived through as a crewmember with some historical evidence of government blundering, allied involvement, and North Korean treachery. We were prisoners of war and are combat veterans. Combining my personal stories with declassified historical records, accounts of espionage, and treason, gives you a comprehensive look at this pivotal moment in our lifetime when many of us were still in our teenage years.

You'll get to know me as a young man from small-town Kansas. It's my story of my own hopes and dreams, coupled with medical issues, deep-dark memories, Post Traumatic Stress Disorder (PTSD), sincere patriotism, dedication to my family, and having experienced much joy and pain during my time on this planet.

Going through the Pueblo Incident changed my life. Of course, I have no idea what my life might have been like if I had not experienced those eleven months. I think about my experience every day; it never goes away. I thank God, my family, countless friends, and many special acquaintances for the support I've received throughout my life. After returning home, I was in my own world, not taking into consideration my loved ones who suffered unimaginably while I was in captivity.

I had a chip on my shoulder after I returned home. I did not understand the anxiety I was experiencing at the time. Thinking there wasn't anything wrong with me, I figured it was just the life one has to deal with. I had quick outbursts of temper when things would not go my way. I understood I was not upset with the people in my life, only myself. Thinking about why I did that, I should do better. But it was not easy.

I distanced myself from my dad. It seemed like we argued over stupid things. Dad did not start the arguments. Tensions eased later, when I eventually received help from the VA, but by that time, my dad had passed away.

I learned a lot from my dad. He had an amazing way of solving problems. Dad's approach to repairs was unconventional. He wasn't one for fancy tools or complicated instructions; his toolbox was more a collection of life experiences and a healthy dose of common sense.

For example, I remember the day I met a brick wall head-on. Lost in a daydream, I never saw the obstacle in my path, and the inevitable collision left my trusty Huffy with a bent front fork and a uselessly turned handlebar. Dejected, I pushed the mangled bike home, a sinking feeling in my stomach. Dad took one look at the damage and a slow smile spread across his face. He flipped the handlebars completely around, so the wheel and handlebars faced in opposite directions.

Then, with a glint of amusement in his eyes, he wheeled the bike outside and purposefully rammed it back into the wall! A gasp escaped my lips, but before I could protest, he straightened the bike back up. And lo and behold, the handlebars turned freely once again, the fork miraculously straightened by the opposing force. It was a testament to Dad's brand of ingenuity—a solution that defied logic yet achieved the desired outcome.

Whether it was a leaky faucet, a broken toy, or a malfunctioning appliance, Dad would approach the problem with a calm demeanor and a twinkle in his eye. There were no explosions or dramatic pronouncements, just a quiet process of analysis, a creative solution formulated, and then the satisfaction of seeing things work as intended once again.

These experiences with Dad instilled in me more than just basic repair skills; they taught me the value of looking at problems from different angles, the importance of resourcefulness, and the confidence to tackle challenges head-on, even if it meant turning the handlebars around and facing them head-first. Dad's legacy wasn't just in the things he fixed, but in the problem-solving approach he taught me—a reminder that sometimes, the simplest solutions are the most effective.

I never expressed my love to Dad for all the wisdom he left me with. He was a very special person in my life, I sure wish I had told him how I felt. All the lessons taught, unknowingly by him, have made it possible for me to live the life I have been blessed to live.

My anxiety still exists but medication takes the edge off. The experience has left me struggling with PTSD and chronic medical issues. VA hospitals rarely put you under for minor surgery, but no surgery is minor for me. I anticipate pain, another one of my PTSD symptoms. I have cold sweats and anxiety, filled with the fear of extreme pain even with local anesthesia.

Surgeries like corrective surgery on both eyes (twice), nasal passage correction, tooth extraction, and cataract surgery may seem minor to most, but these procedures push my anxiety levels to the limits using only local anesthetic.

I have mentally lived with my experience on the Pueblo all my life. It is on my mind every day. No medication will change that.

I found out many years after our release, my mom suffered health issues during and after my captivity. Although my dad did not show any noticeable signs, I am sure he was affected mentally and physically as well.

Two months after my capture, they were told I was wounded. But with the lack of information being released, they had no idea to what extent. All the information the Navy had to pass on was that one crewman was dead and another had lost a leg.

Senator Bob Dole of Kansas kept my folks informed on current events on a regular basis. The press badgered my parents, trying to get a scoop to make headlines. They told them it was their civil duty to let the press know everything they knew about me.

Because of that, I reluctantly talk to the press because what is said is not always interpreted the way I thought it should be. Live interviews make me nervous, but I will occasionally do one if I feel comfortable with the person doing the interview. I never have been able to think fast enough to give a good answer until after the interview.

After being called war heroes and being treated to dinners and parties with Hollywood celebrities upon our return from the hermit kingdom known as North Korea, it was time for us all to start a new way of life. Some remained in the military, some got out. I didn't sulk at my own pity party. I had no job waiting on my return but saw the growing anti-war protests. I just wanted to put all this behind me and get on with my life.

While in captivity for eleven months, the ship's company displayed personal bravery , shouldering the burden of crewing the only United States naval vessel captured by a Communist nation, and still held in captivity. Our crew was locked into circumstances outside our control, enduring harsh cruelty, long days of boredom, stomach churning god-awful food, unsanitary conditions, substandard medical care, and the constant threat of more physical abuse.

The scars I carry, although not noticeable, are a constant reminder of the brutal ordeal I endured in North Korea. The "medical care" I received bordered on barbaric, leaving me with a host of physical and mental injuries. My PTSD anxiety attacks became present for the multiple surgeries I have had over the years. Yet I persevered. Through it all I focused on getting better, on reclaiming my mental state of health, a never-ending battle, but I never gave up.

Maintaining a healthy lifestyle has been a priority ever since. Regular exercise, a balanced diet, and preventive measures like flu shots became my armor against further health battles. And then came COVID-19. We doubled down on our precautions, a testament to our proactive approach to staying well.

Life throws curveballs, that's a given. Cancer, heart issues, accidents—they all loom on the horizon, shades of the unknown.

It wasn't until after my return from captivity that I felt the need to join a church, to find a community of believers. But faith itself has been my anchor since my pre-teen years. It provides solace in times of hardship, hope in the face of uncertainty, and a sense of purpose that transcends the physical world.

Taking life one day at a time allows me to savor the good moments, the simple joys of being alive. That applies to my life in the Navy, and to my personal life before and after the Navy, and it continues to this day.

Despite life's challenges, I choose gratitude. I am truly blessed. My abiding faith has been the bedrock of my existence, a constant source of strength that carried me through the darkest of times.

In captivity, it provided solace in the face of brutality, a flicker of hope that never extinguished. Even after my return, when nightmares and flashbacks threatened to consume me, my faith was a guiding light, leading me back to the path of healing.

Finding a spiritual home at Risen Savior Lutheran Church further enriched my life. Pastor Robert Weinkauf's dedication to Lutheran doctrine and his passionate sermons resonated deeply with me. But it's the sense of community, the unwavering support of my fellow parishioners, that truly makes this church special. We are a family bound by faith, a source of love and encouragement in times of need.

The physical scars may have faded, but the psychological ones serve as a constant reminder of the ordeal I endured. Living with PTSD is a daily battle, a fight against intrusive thoughts and hypervigilance. But I don't face it alone. My faith, wife, family, and friends are my anchor, their love a constant source of strength.

Today, I am a man filled with gratitude. Appreciation for a second chance at life, for the unwavering love of my family and the faith that continues to guide me. As I look toward the future, I do so with a hopeful heart, knowing that with God by my side, and the love of my loved ones surrounding me, I can face whatever challenges come my way.

While captivity undoubtedly impacted each crew member differently, a core truth remains. We were separated from one another, mentally crushed, beaten mercilessly, fed a gut-turning diet, and given substandard medical treatment, all while often isolated from one another.

The worst part of the diet was a soup with a strange look and taste to it. The floating substance had coarse hairlike bristles sticking out of a thick white piece of something. Never had I seen sea urchin cooked. I thought, "Could that be what it is?" Nope.

We learned later that the floating substance was pig fat with hair still attached to the skin, boiled in water, stripped clean of any meat. In the beginning we were never tempted enough to eat the pig fat, but that would change over time, when it was all we were offered.

Captivity's fog can distort memories, even among comrades. It's a testament to the human experience—two different people can witness the same event, yet their recollections vary on exactly what and how events transpired. There have been factual inaccuracies in some other reported accounts of the Pueblo Incident, particularly regarding my injuries. This autobiography will set the record straight.

That is precisely why I was compelled to share my personal story.

The "Declassification of Pueblo Incident" documents undeniably fueled a surge of books on the confrontation. While some accounts differ, what happened to crew members is etched in my memory. My recollections haven't wavered since testifying at the post-release National Security Agency (NSA) interrogation and the Navy Court of Inquiry, which were held immediately following our arrival in the United States, just days after freedom.

Of course, memories are complex. This is a personal story, a testament to life, experiences not easily forgotten but recounted with unwavering honesty.

It's my distinct honor and privilege to know and have served with the crew of the USS Pueblo.

Steven Woelk

Foreword

When you survive the unimaginable alongside another person, a bond forms that transcends ordinary friendship. Steve Woelk and I share such a bond—forged in the crucible of captivity aboard and following the USS Pueblo Incident of 1968, tempered by shared suffering, and strengthened by the quiet courage that emerges when human beings face their darkest hours together.

Steve is a good friend of mine, though "friend" seems an inadequate word to describe someone with whom you've endured what most people cannot fathom. We spent a lot of time together in terrible circumstances that tested the limits of human endurance. Both of us were seriously wounded during the capture of the USS Pueblo, and we shared the traumatic experience of being operated on by North Korean doctors without anesthesia. We endured severe beatings at the hands of the same guards and struggled to survive on the same meager rations of rotten food that barely sustained life.

What many people don't know about Steve—what makes his story particularly remarkable—is that he had no official reason to be where he was during the attack. While still on the ship as North Korean forces closed in, Steve and his friend Duane Hodges were sent by their supervisor to assist those of us tasked with destroying classified materials. I remember Steve later commenting, with that characteristic dry humor that helped us survive those dark days, that he found himself thinking he shouldn't be looking at all this material marked "Top Secret" even as we were frantically burning it.

That simple act of stepping up to help when needed would forever alter the trajectory of both men's lives. Their assistance in our desperate destruction effort cost them both dearly. Duane was killed in the attack, becoming the only American fatality that day, while Steve and I were severely wounded—Steve even more grievously than I. His injuries would leave lasting physical reminders of that day but never dampened his spirit.

Despite spending a year in captivity together—sharing cells, interrogations, the psychological torture of forced confessions, and the daily struggle to maintain our dignity and humanity, I realized when reading this book that there was still so much about Steve I didn't know. His account filled in many blanks for me, revealing dimensions of his character and experiences that even those of us who lived through that ordeal alongside him couldn't fully appreciate.

The USS Pueblo Incident remains one of the most significant and least understood confrontations of the Cold War. Our intelligence vessel was attacked and captured in international waters by North Korean forces on January 23, 1968. The 82 surviving crew members were held as prisoners of war for 11 months before being released on December 23 of that year. But statistics and historical data cannot convey what it meant to live through those events.

Each of the 82 men aboard the Pueblo experienced those 335 days of captivity differently. That's 82 years of collective experience, 82 unique perspectives on what happened before, during, and after our imprisonment. Some stories have been told, others remain private burdens carried by the men who lived them. But I can say with certainty that Steve's account stands among the most honest, insightful, and valuable testimonies to emerge from that chapter of American history.

What makes Steve's story particularly compelling is not just what happened to him, but how he responded to it. Even in our darkest moments of captivity, when hope seemed a luxury we could no longer afford, Steve maintained a quiet resilience that inspired those around him. His ability to endure without surrendering his essential humanity speaks to a strength of character that this book illuminates.

For veterans of the Pueblo Incident, this book will fill in crucial pieces of a puzzle we've spent decades trying to complete. For those unfamiliar with our story, it offers a window into an episode of American history that deserves far more attention than it has received. And for anyone interested in the depths of human endurance and the heights of human courage, Steve's account provides lessons that transcend time and circumstance.

I am honored to introduce this book, not just as a fellow Pueblo survivor, but as someone who witnessed firsthand the events Steve describes and the character he demonstrated throughout our ordeal. His story is not just worth telling, it's essential to understanding both what happened to the men of the USS Pueblo and what it means to maintain one's humanity in the face of inhumane treatment.

This is one account you need to read.

Robert Chicca
USMC
Former POW, USS Pueblo

CHAPTER 1
Prelude to Tension on the High Seas

Before diving into the Pueblo story, I should familiarize you with what happened in South Korea just days before life as we knew it changed forever for the unsuspecting Pueblo crew.

The Association for Diplomatic Studies and Training (ADST) specializes in recording oral testimonies of diplomats in the United States American Foreign Service, which is the diplomatic service of the United States federal government. The US American Foreign Service is responsible for carrying out US foreign policy and represents the interests of the American people abroad. Information outlined here describes the events and circumstances surrounding a major flashpoint between North and South Korea shortly after the USS Pueblo entered the Sea of Japan. Thus, it also sets up the enduring Pueblo story told in this book.

During January 1968, two of the most heinous incidents to unfold on the Korean peninsula since the 1953 Armistice of the Korean War took place. The first involved an assassination attempt on South Korean President Park Chung-Hee by the North Korean government, known as the Blue House Incident. The second was the attack/seizure of the US Navy spy ship, known as the Pueblo Incident. Learning about the former sets up the reasoning behind the latter episode. By understanding the events leading up to the Pueblo Incident, we get a sense for the complex, high-stakes issues that took place in January 1968.

Armed skirmishes had become common along the Korean Demil-
itarized Zone (DMZ) since 1967, but none were more brazen than an
attempt by North Korean commandos to assassinate South Korean
President Park Chung-Hee on the cold night of 21 January, 1968.

An elite North Korean squad of assassins successfully crossed the
DMZ and came within 100 meters of the president's official residence,
called the "Blue House." Their mission, if it had succeeded, would
have certainly reignited open hostilities between the north and south
on the Korean peninsula, and most likely would have drawn the
United States into a second battleground scenario in Southeast Asia.

It is believed by many in the intelligence community that the fail-
ure of this mission may have prompted the North Koreans to seize
the American naval spy ship in anticipation of a retaliatory attack
from South Korea. Pueblo was motoring outside the 12-mile international boundary off the coastal waters of Wonsan, North Korea, as
early as 23 January. Her mission was to gather electronic intelligence
on our long-term enemy. Her sister ship, the USS Banner, had been
on station in the Sea of Japan earlier in the same month with a similar mission and returned to port reporting only minor incidents with
the Russian Navy.

Richard A. Ericson was the US political counselor in Seoul, South
Korea, at the time and much of the following story is from his oral
history.

BLUE HOUSE RAID

"To [South] Koreans, the Blue House raid was the most critical
event during that 1965-68 period, because it came at the culmination
of a long series of incidents on Korean territory. People were very
tense and South Korean President Park used this tension to justify
many of his repressive measures. He was very fond of referring to
President (Abraham) Lincoln's suspension of habeas corpus to jus-

Cheongwadae Blue House

tify his actions when speaking to all U.S. congressmen who came through, protesting his repressive measures.

"Park Chung-Hee was growing increasingly frustrated with his perceived weakening position in Korea, due to his support of American involvement in the Vietnam War. He was also walking a tight rope by seeking increased US military aid for South Korea.

"Now, rumors began emerging about a group of heavily armed North Korean infiltrators spotted within the DMZ. After threatening residents in a local village, these infiltrators vanished without a trace. This sighting further escalated tensions, prompting the South Korean government to implement heightened security measures and launch a massive military search operation.

"For two days they were not heard from. Then, on the frigid night of January 21st, a group of men dressed in South Korean military uniforms emerged from the North and marched toward a police checkpoint near the Blue House.

"This checkpoint had been established specifically to detect these infiltrators. When they approached, South Korean police challenged them. However, their leader employed North Korean tactics and ordered the South Korean officer to stand down, claiming to be members of the Republic of Korea Military Intelligence (ROK CIC) returning from a mission. He arrogantly dismissed the police, suggesting they should know better than to interfere with a military operation. And, of course, the police backed off. One of the police officers was irritated with the arrogant demeanor of the group. He decided to radio headquarters and report the encounter. Headquarters, however, had no record of any CIC operations in the area. At the Blue House, a police lieutenant alerted by the radio transmission decided to personally investigate the situation.

"The commando squad, now within 800 yards of the Blue House, slipped into a densely populated area. When challenged by this police lieutenant, they opened fire immediately, killing the policeman and several bus passengers who happened to be in the wrong place at the wrong time. Despite the proximity to their target, these North Koreans lacked a coherent plan as they dispersed into small groups without any apparent contingencies. They evidently thought they could march right into the Blue House compound, looking like South Korean soldiers and carry out their suicide mission."

Ericson went on to say, "To make a long story short, they split into small groups and the ROK devoted enormous resources to rounding them up. They captured two almost immediately, two more just disappeared and were never heard from again, and the rest were all killed in fire fights with ROK security forces. Of the two they captured, one was taken to the local police station and once inside, he managed to detonate a grenade concealed on his person, killing himself and about five senior South Korean police officials. They didn't shake him down very well, obviously. But the other one, after severe interrogation, broke down and told all about himself and his unit.

"We were not aware that there were units of this kind, but the captured spy said there was an organization of at least a thousand people currently undergoing training in North Korea for just such missions. The South Korean military had never heard of anything like this, so they asked him where they had trained. He told where the camp was and drew a map of its layout. When the spy plane photographs were developed, the camp was where he said it was and his map was almost an exact overlay of the photos."

The police then asked him whether these units used radio during their training and his answer was a resounding, "Yes." He gave them frequencies to which the ROK denied ever having heard anything on these. He said to try again, and up they came.

Ericson continues, "So we began to believe this guy. He said that their primary mission was to assassinate President Park. They were supposed to deploy not very far from where they had been intercepted. Their idea was to rush the Blue House, raise hell, and kill Park." He also said that their original mission had been to split into three groups, one of which was to go to the American military headquarters at Yong-san and kill the UN Forces Commander along with other senior officers such as the UN representative to the Armistice Commission. The third group was to come into American Embassy Compound One, kill the ambassador and anybody else they could lay their hands on.

"We believed him. Actually, the girl's high school sat right next to the wall of that embassy compound and had a very large open play area. A new building was being constructed right alongside the wall, where a lot of construction materials were piled. We had armed security guards, but they weren't trusted all that much. The ambassador then issued a weapon to each family in Compound One and the UN Command designated a platoon of tanks to stand by and come to the rescue should the North Koreans return. Tank crews were billeted in the Yong-san post gymnasium, thus depriving soldiers and high school kids of their basketball court. The tanks got lost trying to find the compound during the one attempt they made of a dry run on the trial rescue effort. But the general knowledge that they were there was reassuring to some."

DUMP THE NORTH KOREAN CORPSES ON
THE CONFERENCE TABLE

Later in his oral recap, Ericson says, "Park went ape over this incident. It came close. It clearly demonstrated that his phobia of assassination was well-grounded, and he reacted by doing what he occasionally did during periods of great stress. He disappeared up to his mountain retreat with a couple of friends and a couple of ladies and a large supply of alcohol. But we heard stories that he was enraged, beside himself, out of control!"

South Koreans looked at this assassination threat to their president as a major event. Ericson says, "We were seriously concerned that out of that mountain retreat of his would come the order to go get them, cross the DMZ and seek retaliation of some kind. But he was out of touch."

Meanwhile, the ROK security forces were hunting down the remaining spies and finally caught all but one.

Remember the one prisoner who told his story? He commanded the assault element, which would secure the first floor, allowing the rest of the team to proceed upstairs and kill Park. Lt. Kim Shin-jo revealed in an interview with NBC News on the 50th anniversary of the day he crossed the DMZ into South Korea.

Ericson continues his testimony, "The way they broke him was to line up all the dead bodies of his comrades on a hillside, a single file of twenty-seven corpses in various states of disrepair, then marched this prisoner along the line. He was still refusing to talk. But when his ROK escorts reached the last body, they kicked the head. As the lone remaining spy watched that head roll off down the hill, he decided to tell all. Responding in a huff of confident defiance, some ROK generals felt that if they weren't going to declare war on North Korea, they should at least haul the corpses up to Panmunjom, flay the North Koreans verbally, dump the bodies on the conference table and storm out of the building. However, calmer heads eventually prevailed.

"Just days after the Blue House raid, the Pueblo was seized and that is where we really got into trouble with the South Koreans, as they had no knowledge we had a spy ship there, or that the USS Banner was off the coast on similar duty earlier in the month."

The Blue House raid was never duplicated, but the North Korean commandos succeeded in making everyone nervous. The tensions rising from this incident nearly sparked another major armed conflict in Southeast Asia at the same time the US military was deeply engaged in battling communist armies 2,158 miles away in Vietnam. Strained relations, as we will see between the US and South Korea, could not have come at a worse time in history.

CHAPTER 2
Seizure

The Pueblo was a very small Baltic Class coastal freighter, slow and most inefficient. It was not a weaponized US Navy ship of war. Except for a few small arms, Pueblo was a sad excuse for a US Navy vessel. But this ship was one of the Navy's electronic intelligence gathering vessels, along with the USS Banner and USS Palm Beach. Pueblo was on her maiden mission, fairly new on the job, patrolling up and down the coast of North Korea in the Sea of Japan, and picking up anything it could by way of North Korean electronic activity. The North Korean Navy knew it was there. However, if the UN Commander in Chief may have known it was there, the US Ambassador was not informed, and neither were the South Koreans.

Soon after the failed Blue House raid, Pueblo was approached by North Korean patrol boats off the port of Wonsan. It was pretty clearly not in what the North Koreans considered coastal waters. The ship's orders were to remain in international waters, past the internationally accepted twelve-mile limit. The North Koreans certainly tolerated it, probably not wanting to kick up a major fuss. But when Park survived the assassination attempt, North Korea seized the opportunity to prepare for a retaliatory strike by taking out the US spy ship.

North Korea was fearful that since they failed to kill Park, he might order some kind of major hostile response and they didn't want a vessel with this kind of listening capability sitting just off the

Army freighter before becoming USS Pueblo. US Army photo

coast, giving advantages to the enemy. It was something to get out of the way."

Prior to these two incidents, the North Korean Navy conducted a series of South Korean boat seizures on the high seas with impunity and regularity. It was their habit to pick up South Korean fishing boats, hijack their crews, brainwash them, and send them back to South Korea. There had probably been 50 to 100 separate incidents of that kind. It turns out that seizure of the USS Pueblo meant a great deal more to the US than the Blue House raid, and in South Korea the reverse was true.

Three nations were tensing up. North Korea failed to assassinate the South Korean President and lost almost all of its would-be assassins in the process. South Korea became incensed over their most feared enemy's aggressive actions. And the United States lost a Naval intelligence gathering ship and crew on the high seas.

Interestingly, South Korea was upset over the fact that Pueblo was there in the first place; and the icing on the cake was that South Korea would be shut out of any negotiations between the US and North Korea while China would be at North Korea's side throughout all talks.

One of the major points of difficulty with the South Koreans was that they thought the Blue House raid was the most critical issue. As this all began to unfold, the South Korean leadership treated Pueblo as a sideshow.

Ericson opines, "Back in the United States, Americans, from Lyndon Johnson down the chain of command, thought that the Pueblo seizure was the most heinous crime of the century, and the Blue House raid was something few had heard about."

That must have become a real bone of contention. Washington reacted violently to the Pueblo capture, and Johnson ordered the carrier USS Enterprise to steam up the east coast of Korea from Japan, take up an offensive posture off the coast of Wonsan and impose a threatening posture against the North Koreans. Ericson went on to say, "Some thought it was about taking out Wonsan and all its defenses, then recapturing the ship. Perhaps it was simply to intimidate the North Koreans into consenting to whatever demands we might make for reparations. All kinds of wild ideas were floated about how the US should respond. Our main concern in the embassy was trying to get Washington to focus on the fact that there was a real problem with the South Koreans because of the Blue House raid, the disparity between our reaction to it and that of the Pueblo seizure. We were not concerned as much with the North Koreans, who probably were not interested in a real war at that time but who would certainly respond if attacked."

THE SOUTH KOREANS WERE MORE EMOTIONAL
THAN RATIONAL

That, of course, was why the United States sent the carrier Enterprise into North Korean waters. A cold assessment of the situation estimated that it would take everything the Enterprise had and probably a good deal more to penetrate the air envelope around Wonsan. We might very well have found ourselves facing a full-scale war in Korea if we tried to do anything of that kind.

Political Counselor Ericson's own feeling was, "If we had attacked Wonsan, it would have encouraged Park to the point where he might just order South Korean forces to go on the offensive–UN commander or no UN commander. The man was out of touch with reality during this whole period. So we had to figure out how to get the ship and the crew back," within this backdrop of spiraling international intrigue.

Continuing in his report, Ericson says, "The South Koreans were more emotional than rational, and many of them already looked at the US reaction as timid. Of course, they weren't aware that the forces we had in Korea at the time—two divisions—were in very bad shape and probably not combat-ready. They had about two-thirds of their complement of troops, the shortfall being made up by KATUSAs [Korea Augmentations to the U.S. Army]."

Going back to the Blue House incident, the North Korean raiders had deliberately come right through the US Army's 2nd Division lines. The captured assassin said, "They couldn't get through the South Korean side because the South Koreans did their patrolling, kept awake, did not smoke cigarettes on the line, did not huddle together for warmth and all that kind of thing. Whereas, the Americans up along the DMZ smoked. You could smell their smoke; you could hear them talking. They huddled together when it got very, very cold and they relied on electronic sensors installed at American positions."

But a lot of these sensors—anti-personnel radar, seismic detectors, and stuff like that—had been developed for battle in the warmer climate of Vietnam. No one made sure they functioned as well when the temperature sank to twenty degrees below zero. And malfunction they did.

The US 2nd Division commander was furious when he heard the North Korean spy say they came right through his lines. They took him up to the big chain link fence along the entire front of the 2nd Division's lines and the commander said, "Prove it to me." The Korean spy walked up to the fence at the point where he indicated they had penetrated, kicked it, and watched a large section of fence fall out. He knew exactly where to go, so this certainly enhanced his credibility.

It's interesting to note that they had taken two days to come down through the hills undetected, with temperatures way below freezing all day and all night. It was a marvelous feat of endurance, carrying all their equipment over rough and mountainous terrain in vicious winter weather and getting to Seoul through the American defenses so fast.

THE SOUTH KOREANS WERE FURIOUS

"Now," Ericson continues, "how we get the crew of the Pueblo back became our main concern. But to US staff in Seoul, placating the South Koreans was just as important, and, of course, tactics used in getting the crew back made the South Koreans angrier. The embassy wasn't really consulted very much.

"The powers that be in Washington decided once it became clear that negotiations with the North Koreans were possible, they should be held at Panmunjom. The North Koreans, with their own objectives in mind, wanted Panmunjom. Washington decided to use the United Nations Command representative to the Military Armistice Com-

South Korean (ROK) Security at Panmunjom

mission, U.S. Navy Rear Admiral John Victor Smith and his American staff, who spearheaded the initial negotiations at Panmunjom."

Panmunjom has been called a village, but it is not and never was a village; it is just an inn. It is a full-fledged armistice meeting place, and it was regarded as neutral territory. It was close to the scene, with good communications for both the North Koreans and the United States and therefore was the optimal location. The problem with the South Koreans is that they regarded it as their territory.

The US team would negotiate directly with the North Koreans and no other nation represented in the UN Command would be present. We wouldn't take any of the UN Command members. Most specifically, we wouldn't take any South Koreans. The North Koreans had the Chinese with them for every meeting from the very beginning.

When word of US intentions reached the South Koreans, they erupted emotionally. When their initial protests were delivered to Ambassador Bill Porter, he treated them with a quick and dismissive attitude, and this enraged them to the point that they refused to talk to him. We went ahead.

At first, Lyndon Johnson called all the shots personally. He was on the telephone a few times while the Enterprise was there. The State

Department quickly set up an inter-agency crisis team. The South Koreans were absolutely furious and suspicious of what we might do. They anticipated that the North Koreans would try to exploit the situation to the ROK's disadvantage in every way possible. They were rapidly growing distrustful of the US and losing faith in their great ally.

Of course, we had this other problem to ensure that the ROK would not retaliate for the Blue House raid to ease their growing feelings of insecurity. They began to realize that the DMZ was porous and they wanted more equipment and aid, which came from the United States. Ericson says, "So, we were juggling a few problems and demands. Once the venue for the negotiations was agreed on with Pyongyang, we had to find solutions for our problems with the South Koreans. Park, by this time, had returned to Seoul."

A BRIEF HISTORY OF US-NORTH KOREA RELATIONS

The United States and North Korean relations have been historically tense, marked by periods of crises and intermittent diplomacy ever since aggressive hostilities ceased between the two nations in 1953.

The Korean War (1950-1953) was a major conflict that pitted North Korea, supported by China and the Soviet Union, against South Korea, supported by the United States and other United Nations member states. The war ended in a stalemate, with signing of the armistice agreement in 1953. This was not a peace treaty, which remains an open issue. Hostilities ceased. The DMZ between North and South Korea was formally established. The war did not officially end, leaving the Korean Peninsula technically still in a state of war. By those terms, it remains America's longest-running war. The North and the South remain on edge with each other.

Following the Korean War cessation of hostilities, relations between the two countries remained manageably hostile. North Korea pursues a policy of isolationism, developing nuclear weapons and ballistic missile programs, continuing to threaten South Korea. Large numbers of US troops remain stationed near the DMZ, holding a tenuous peace.

FIRST MISSION

The USS Pueblo was originally assigned to "Operation Clickbeetle." However, in the autobiography, *Bucher*, written by Commander Lloyd Bucher, he states, "The Navy wanted Operation Clickbeetle focused on the USSR, its biggest maritime rival. But when it became clear, after half a dozen voyages, that the Banner was acquiring high-quality intelligence, the National Security Agency began lobbying for the ships itinerary to be broadened to include China and North Korea.

Captain Lloyd Bucher, US Navy photo

Navy officials objected, saying that doing so would negate Clickbeetle's central premise: that American ferrets would be protected by the gentlemen's agreement between the United States and the Soviet Union that neither would harm the other's boats for fear of reciprocal action. China and North Korea were bound by no such constraints. They possessed only coast-hugging navies, incapable of ranging far enough from shore to eavesdrop on foreign adversaries. Thus, they had less to lose by going after American snoopers. But the NSA prevailed in the debate."

We left port on our first mission in January 1968. I had no idea what our mission was or where we were headed. I did not need to

> *Although Lloyd Bucher's official naval rank*
> *was Commander, as the CO of the USS Pueblo,*
> *he is the Captain.*

know these things. I suppose the mission of Pueblo should have been obvious with all the antennas sticking out all over the place, but we really did not pay much attention. We were along for the ride wherever we went, learning skills and building friendships.

I just did my job standing watches, following orders, doing what I was told to do. My normal duty watch was monitoring the evaporator in the auxiliary engine room. The evaporator used steam to convert sea water into potable water for the ship. Another duty of the engine room cronies was to take fuel and water soundings in the tanks below deck. These soundings would determine how much would have to be transferred from one tank to another to maintain ballast for the ship's stability. We would have to remove a cap located outside on the deck, drop a weighted tape measuring device down the hole, then retrieve it to record the levels.

Stepping out on the open deck in the dark of night with the ship rocking up, down and sideways, all I could think about was, "What if I were to be swept overboard?" We carried these little lights on our life jackets that would come on automatically if we lost our balance and were accidentally tossed overboard. The lights were intended for the rescuers to be able to locate us in the water. No matter what precautions you took, the chances of being recovered from the cold sea at night were slim to none. I also carried a flashlight to make darn sure someone in the pilot house knew I was outside on the wet deck and would keep an eye on me.

Being at sea had its pros and cons. Some days the water would be like a sheet of glass but most of the time it was rough. We motored through fog, rain, freezing rain, and a rarity at sea, snow.

Occasionally, after a night of heavy swells and waves breaking over the handrailing, several fish could be found on the deck. The two Filipino stewards on board would gather them up to cook for themselves.

Going back to the time we left Bremerton, Washington, we would see an array of fish, dolphins, killer whales, and sharks, but the most interesting were the flying fish. They would swim fast to gain momentum to come out of the water, spread their clear wings and glide. When they would start to settle down to the water, they would wiggle their tail to stay aloft as long as they could. They did not go very high but could sail quite a distance before dropping back into the sea.

There were thirty communication technicians (CTs) on board, but I did not know their purpose for being there. I was young and from the Midwest. What did I know or care to know about these things? The CTs never associated with us, and we never associated with them.

A small generator located in the Auxiliary Generator Engine room supplied a dedicated power supply to the Special Operations Department, the "SOD HUT" located directly above on the main deck. A mysterious device was located in the auxiliary engine room, but I had no idea what it was used for. We learned early on to not ask questions on Pueblo. This device was located in a waterproof compartment, four feet square rising from the deck of the ship up to around six feet in height. The space was insulated with a water-tight hatch large enough for a person to crawl inside. Located in this space was a six-inch wide, one-inch thick, tapered, double-edged blade contraption extending through a water-tight seal in the hull of the ship. We were instructed to open the hatch every watch to make sure the compartment was dry, and, if any water was present, pump it out.

At one of our ship's reunions, following our repatriation to the US, I asked one of the CTs what this might be used for. He explained it had something to do with the oceanographers' research. All of us who stood watch together never talked about it, we just knew we had to inspect the space on each watch.

January was cold enough to freeze ice on everything exposed outside. The deckhands would have to knock the ice off all the metal surfaces. I was thankfully never part of the ice-removing crew.

We went through our daily routines cleaning spaces, doing what we were told to do. The only two major issues evident to me were the continuous steering problems and one of the main engines may have needed an overhaul.

I had no interest in having anything to do with the engines, working on diesel engines or doing anything associated with them. I had pretty much made up my mind to be an electrician long ago, no matter how long it would take. Maybe that was an unconscious desire to follow in my dad's line of work.

CHAPTER 3
"Operation Clickbeetle"

The Banner class coastal freighter was a category of three environmental research ships converted from Camano-class cargo ships by the United States Navy during the 1960s. The class comprised three ships: the Banner, the Pueblo, and the Palm Beach. The ships were originally US Army vessels, which had been built in 1944. Although officially classified as environmental research ships, they were assigned to intelligence gathering as part of the Auxiliary General Environmental Research program (AGER).

In 1964, the Department of Defense (DOD) became interested in having smaller, less expensive, and more flexible and responsive signals intelligence collection vessels than the existing AGTR and T-AG vessels. The mothballed light cargo ships were the most suitable existing DOD ships.

The National Security Agency (NSA) wanted twenty-five AGER vessels, though, after a detailed discussion with the Navy, the budget request reduced the number to fifteen for what the NSA called the Phase I and Phase II Trawler program. Eventually, only three were converted.

Commander Bucher writes in his autobiography, *Bucher*, "Five days before Christmas, the USS Banner—the first spy ship sent out under Operation Clickbeetle—returned to Yokosuka from its latest patrol and tied up next to the Pueblo. After several weeks at sea, the

Banner's unshaven crew looked like tired pirates. Bucher and his men soon would replace them in the wintry Sea of Japan."

The USS Pueblo's mission was to surveil high-frequency electronic emissions with line-of-sight propagation requiring operating closer to shore than previous intelligence gathering missions. Pueblo was originally unarmed, but the crew of eighty-three were issued five M1911 pistols and three M1 Garand rifles. Banner, during her mission, was confronted by Soviet Navy ships while operating off the Pacific coast of the Soviet Union. These ships would sometimes display international signal flags meaning: "Heave to or I will fire," but the Banner kept steaming with scrupulous attention to International Regulations for Preventing Collisions at Sea. Soviet recognition of possible American reciprocity against Soviet ships on similar missions discouraged attacks.

The cargo ship was transferred from DOD to the United States Navy on 12 April, 1966, and renamed USS Pueblo, after the city and county of Pueblo, Colorado, on 18 June of the same year. Initially, she was classified as a light cargo ship for basic refitting at Puget Sound Naval Shipyard during 1966. Pueblo was prepared under a non-secret cover as a light cargo ship, and the general crew staff

USS Pueblo at sea, US Navy photo

training followed this strategy. Forty-four percent of the crew had never been to sea when first assigned.

Installation of signals intelligence equipment, at a cost of $1.5 million, was delayed to 1967 for budgetary reasons. She resumed service as what is colloquially known as a "spy ship" and redesignated AGER-2 on 13 May, 1967. The limited budget for conversion caused denial of several improvements requested by the incoming Commanding Officer (CO), Commander Lloyd Bucher. The requested engine overhaul was denied, despite sister ship Banner's experience of drifting for two days along with an inability to communicate after both engines failed on patrol. Think of it—a Navy spy ship unable to maneuver and unable to communicate. The emergency scuttling system request was declined, and Bucher was subsequently not allowed to obtain explosives for demolition charges, which would be needed in the event of enemy encroachment.

These were needed in the event the ship was confronted by an enemy power, which, in fact, took place. A replacement of "burn barrels," with a fuel-fed incinerator to allow speedy destruction of classified documents, was also denied. After Bucher's subsequent request to reduce the ship's library bulk of classified publications was similarly denied, he managed to purchase a less-capable incinerator using some discretionary funds originally intended for crew comfort. That equipment would ultimately prove to be inadequate.

Following the USS Liberty Incident on 8 June, Vice Chief of Naval Operations (VCNO) Horacio Rivero Jr. ordered that no Navy ship would operate without adequate means of defending itself. VCNO staff directed the shipyard to install a 3-inch/50-caliber gun on Pueblo's main deck, with provisions for ammunition storage, but Bucher successfully argued against such installation because of reduced ship stability by addition of this weight above the main deck.

To put that in context, the USS Liberty Incident was an attack on a United States Navy technical research ship (otherwise known as a spy ship) by an Israeli Air Force jet fighter aircraft and Israeli Navy motor torpedo boats, on 8 June 1967, during the "Six-Day War." So two US Navy spy ships were attacked by foreign powers, in similar fashion, within a period of seven months.

One was by an ally and one was by an adversary, perhaps utilizing their lessons learned from the Liberty incident. The combined air and sea attack on the Liberty killed thirty-four crew members (naval officers, seamen, two marines, and one civilian NSA employee), wounding 171, and severely damaging the ship.

At the time, the Liberty was in international waters north of the Sinai Peninsula, about 25.5 nautical miles (47.2 km; 29.3 mi) northwest from the Egyptian city of Arish. Israel eventually apologized for the attack, saying that the USS Liberty had been attacked in error after being mistaken for an Egyptian ship. Both the Israeli and US governments conducted inquiries and issued reports that concluded the attack was a mistake, due to Israeli confusion about the ship's identity.

The USS Pueblo was 177 feet in length, with a 32-foot beam and a nine-foot draft. Flank speed was approximately fifteen knots. The keel was laid in Kewaunee, Wisconsin, in 1944.

In another reference to the book, *Bucher*, like her sister ship Banner, a onetime freighter, the Pueblo had ferried coconuts, pigs and pregnant women around the Mariana Islands for years. "In 1965, workmen at Bremerton converted (Banner) into a spy platform in just seven weeks—so fast that one Navy officer observed that it had been 'literally put together like a plate of hash.' When Navy ships are not being utilized, they are either placed in the mothball fleet or dismantled. The Pueblo was taken from the Navy's mothball fleet, then towed to Bremerton where it was retrofitted—in just under two months—for its future duty in the Pacific Fleet. A hastily prepared ship for a mission she was never built to handle.

Pueblo's new mission required construction of a new communication room to hold all the surveillance equipment. We called it the "SOD HUT." Racks on the deck outside held equipment used by the oceanographers along with an array of antennas for intelligence gathering and communication. Berthing quarters were added to accommodate eighty-three crewmen, forty more than designed for a ship of this size.

USS PUEBLO
[AKL-44]

USS PALM BEACH
[AKL-45]

PUGET SOUND NAVAL SHIPYARD
Bremerton, Washington

13 MAY 1967

Commissioning, Steven Woelk photo

Aboard were the ship's crew of five officers and thirty-eight enlisted men, plus one officer and thirty-seven enlisted men of the NSA, plus two civilian oceanographers providing a cover story. In May 1967, the USS Palm Beach and the USS Pueblo were re-commissioned together at the same ceremony in Bremerton.

The USS Banner had already been commissioned and was engaged in its Southeast Asia spy mission. Palm Beach would be sent to the Atlantic Fleet. The missions of all three ships were set in place by the National Security Agency (NSA) out of Ft. Meade, Maryland.

MY INTRODUCTION TO PUEBLO

When my leave ended after boot camp, it was time to start the next stage of my Navy life. I flew out of Kansas City to Seattle, Washington, in January 1967. This time I was traveling alone, duffle bag slung over my shoulder and scared half to death about what to expect or how I would even get to my ship after stepping off the plane.

For starters, my scheduled flight from the Kansas City downtown airport had to be canceled due to low visibility. In the early 60s the Kansas City International Airport (MCI) was being built north of downtown Kansas City, while daily air traffic was still handled out of the old downtown airport. MCI was not officially in operation, but the tower and runways were operational and had the capability of handling instrument arrivals and departures. All passengers from downtown canceled flights were bused to MCI. Since the terminals were not operational, they took us directly to the plane by bus, using passenger boarding stairs to access the plane.

After an uneventful flight, we landed in Seattle. I took public transportation to the Bremerton Ferry dock and caught the one-hour ferry ride to Bremerton from Seattle via Puget Sound. The dock was within walking distance of the Navy Shipyard, so after walking

USS Pueblo, dockside, Steven Woelk photo

through the main gate, I took a military shuttle bus to my barracks. My orders were to report to a transit barracks, where I would be spending the night before reporting to the ship the following morning.

This was exciting! My first shipboard duty station. My senses were on high alert, this was a totally new experience for me.

Following my orders, the next day I reported to the USS Palm Beach, which was docked at the pier next to the USS Pueblo. I remember walking on board the Palm Beach and seeing a ship looking like it had been through a disaster. Wires were hanging from the overhead, it was unpainted inside and out, with a rusty hull and a lot of the equipment yet to be installed. Overall, it was a general mess. It was not ready for crews to move aboard.

I held the rank of Fireman E-2, and I would be assigned to the department keeping the ship's operating systems in good working order. I let it be known that I wished to be an electrician, although I had no electrical training whatsoever. The Electrician's Mate was in need of a striker, a naval term for apprentice. So I got lucky and was on my way, or so I thought. I do not know what happened behind the scenes, but as fate would have it, they soon relieved me of that position and transferred me to another ship—the Pueblo—undergoing the same retrofit as the Palm Beach.

Pueblo looked the same inside and out, not fit for duty at the time, but it did appear to be a little further along in the repairs. What I didn't know at the time was that both ships were being redesigned and refitted to handle their new mission, intelligence gathering.

Although their missions would be similar, they would be operating in different parts of the world. The Palm Beach would go to the Atlantic fleet while Pueblo would be sent to the Pacific fleet.

During my stay in the barracks, I met some really good guys from the USS Sterett, DDG-104. The Sterett was a newly built Guided Missile Destroyer, soon to be commissioned and sent on its way. Several guys stationed aboard her invited me to the ship's commissioning party held at one of the local parks outside of Bremerton. There were several hundred people at the party enjoying beer and food around a large open pit fire. Steaks and fresh salmon were either cooked on a grill or smoked on cedar planks in the pit. It was the first time I had ever had the opportunity to eat fresh salmon instead of from a can. I had never tasted any better fish than salmon on that day. As a testimony to the salmon, it went fast while there were still plenty of steaks left over for any beef lovers.

While in the barracks, most of us played penny-ante poker to pass time. We ate, slept, and spent much of our off time in the barracks together, being too poor to do much of anything else. Slot-car racing was popular back then, so several of the guys had their slot cars with them. A slot car track found at an arcade in downtown Bremerton was where we would go to race. It was good, cheap, fun entertainment for poor sailors without a car.

Sailors assigned to the barracks would take turns on mess duty or KP, a common abbreviation for "kitchen police." The dining hall and kitchen were located in a different building, and while on KP we were required to move into the dining hall barracks. There wasn't very much happening aboard ship, so keeping busy helped to pass time more quickly. One of our KP jobs involved taking turns mopping and waxing the barracks berthing area tile floor. It was a large area with bunk beds filling the entire space, not an easy cleaning job for one person.

If you managed to do a good job waxing, you would get a day off from kitchen duties. Like any military building it's cleaned over and over, so unless someone made a mess it was easy to make it look good with very little effort. It was supposed to be dusted, mopped, waxed, and buffed each time it was cleaned. I thought if I dusted the floor really well, waxed only the areas where the sun would shine on the floor, it would look like a mirror when finished. It worked and the floor looked fantastic! I earned a day off from KP. But the fickle finger of fate stepped in once more and just before my scheduled day off, we were called to move aboard the Pueblo permanently.

WELCOMING THE NEW CREW ON BOARD
THE USS PUEBLO

The Pueblo was now operational with new crewmen arriving daily. Our berthing quarters had new bunks with new sheets and blankets. Everything had a fresh smell; everything had been painted. It looked like a real Navy ship.

The galley was open for business and the crew was eating on board. At night, several of us would either go downtown to Bremerton or get some beer for a party on the outskirts of town. Several of my friends from the West Coast had their personal cars with them, so we were able to leave the base and venture out. For a small-town boy from the Kansas countryside, this was a whole new experience. We would go to the south side of Dyes Inlet where the scenery was beautiful with the Olympic Mountains, which are the most prominent range visible from Bremerton, off in the distance. They form a stunning backdrop to the city and Puget Sound. It was a perfect place to park, drink, shoot the bull, and stay out of trouble. Sometimes we would find a secluded fire trail where we could get far away from society.

Fortunately, all the friends I hung out with were twenty-one or older. Since I was only 19, I relied on them to get the beer. Olympia or Rainier beer were the beverages of choice. Coors was the best choice where I came from but wouldn't you know it? Coors would have to be bootlegged in if we wanted it for our parties.

Seattle had a few inexpensive and interesting places to see if you used the transportation systems. The monorail was built for the 1962 World's Fair to carry people from downtown to the Seattle Center, where exhibitions and the Space Needle were located. The monorail was within walking distance from the Bremerton Ferry Dock. A couple times I ventured out alone to attend a concert at the Seattle Center. I saw the comedy duo Homer and Jethro, and Waylon Jennings and his band. The concerts would start so late in the evening there was not enough time to see the entire show, catch the last ferry to Bremerton and get back to the ship the next day before roll call.

We made so little money back then we could hardly make it from paycheck to paycheck. We made enough to buy the essentials to live on, but toward the end of the pay period we could not afford to go out.

Meeting girls in Bremerton was challenging, unless you were one of the guys who had a car. Those guys obviously had more than just a sailor's income to get around. Sailors were not very popular, though most of their parents and relatives worked on the Navy base. I did not have an outgoing personality, so it was difficult for me to talk to girls even if I would have had wheels to get around.

One of my best friends on the Pueblo was Duane Hodges from Creswell, Oregon, a three-hour drive down the coast. He had his personal car with him, which made it easy to get around. One weekend, Duane invited me to go with him to visit his family and friends in his hometown. It would be a long drive so we could only spend one night before turning around and heading back. While in Creswell, Duane showed me the saw mill where his family and he worked before he entered the Navy. He introduced me to his mom and dad, who were extremely nice to me, just like Duane. Our moms exchanged letters up until my mom's death in 1999.

Looking back on my experience as a Pueblo crew member, I'm proud to say that I am an original plank owner of the USS Pueblo (AKL-44) later redesignated AGER-2.

In the US Navy, to "own a plank" means to be a member of the first crew to serve aboard a newly commissioned ship. The term comes from the idea that these sailors were present when the ship was being built and essentially owned a piece of the ship's deck (a plank). While ships today are rarely built with wooden decks, the term "plank own-

Plank owner, Steven Woelk photo

er" still holds significant prestige. It signifies a unique connection to the ship and its history. Plank owners often receive special recognition and may be eligible for unique memorabilia or privileges related to the ship.

The Pueblo Plank is a finished piece of 4" x 8" wood with an inscription that reads "Plank Owner USS Pueblo AKL-44, 13 May 1967." In the middle of the Plank is an etching of the USS Pueblo emblem.

Captain Bucher's superiors were present for the festivities, as well as many family members of crewmen who were in the area.

TIME TO DEVELOP OUR SEA LEGS

With a couple of short sea voyages under our belts, it was time to get underway to start our Navy adventure and develop our sea legs down the coast.

After testing and deficiency rework, Pueblo sailed from Bremerton shipyard to a pier in San Francisco. Two days later, we were out to sea once again, headed for San Diego shake-down training on 11 September, 1967. These tests were necessary to see what the ship was capable of doing after refitting.

CHAPTER 4
Pueblo on the High Seas

Pueblo was a very rough riding ship, even though we stayed within sight of shore. It was not designed as a seagoing vessel, so sailing across the ocean would prove to be very interesting. Many of the crew got sick from the constant rolling waves. Some said they never did but were seen heaving their guts over the rail. It was not uncommon to walk down the corridor of the ship and step in vomit. If the rough seas did not make you sick the salt air and smell of bile would.

When you saw a crew member making a mad dash toward the hatch leading outside, you knew he had the urge to get sick. Sometimes they made it all the way to the rail, sometimes they did not.

Outside in the fresh air, I felt okay. Working down in the main engine room where the temperatures reached over 100 degrees, was exhausting. The smell of fumes from hot fuel and oil at times was just too much for me. I would get sick along with all the others, but for very different reasons. If I could sit on the ladder in front of a large vent blowing fresh air into the engine room, I would feel fine.

When the seas were rough, I could swear the engines were moving up and down as the ship rocked back and forth. There were times when you felt it would be easier walking on the walls instead of the deck. Rough seas took some getting used to, but after a while you get used to it enough to walk around the ship. You develop "swabby" sea legs by learning to anticipate the roll of the waves and corresponding roll of the ship. Later, the stretch from Bremerton to San Diego was the only time I ever got seasick, but not enough to go to the handrail. That time I managed to make it to the head.

One of the CTs got sick as soon as we left Bremerton. He could be found in the head hugging the toilet 24/7. A communication tech in this condition would be no help to contribute to the mission of the ship, so he was transferred off the boat. He was the lucky one.

Steaming into San Francisco Bay, our first port was Treasure Island, where we spent a couple of days for repairs. My friend and I had shore leave so we decided to hit a bar downtown. Now as I mentioned earlier, I was only nineteen, so my chances of getting served were slim. We entered the front door and sat down at the bar.

My friend told me to relax, "Order what you want, and they will not question your age." I decided to order what I thought would be an appropriate drink for any adult, a scotch and Coke. The bartender looked at me with a smirk on his face, then turned to my friend and said, "He's not 21, is he?" He must have felt sorry for me, because that was my first drink served in a bar, even if it was a complete waste of scotch.

San Francisco was an experience to remember, sailing under the Golden Gate Bridge. Another shipmate of mine, Rich, lived in Sebastopol, California. When I drove to California to visit him in the 1970s, we drove across that most magnificent bridge. Now I can say I have traveled over and under the Golden Gate Bridge.

Sailing further down the coast, we reached San Diego a little early, before there was room at the pier, so we sat, bobbing up and down, off the coast until a ship left and we were granted space.

The Pueblo's only armament consisted of two 50-caliber machine guns mounted on an open handrail fore and aft. When the 50s were mounted in Bremerton, there was little time to train anyone in their operation. So, Captain Bucher took advantage of this delay to get some sailors much-needed hands-on training, handling and firing the guns. Our Gunner's Mate and several crewmen were responsible to ready the guns to be fired. A couple of empty 55-gallon steel drums were tossed overboard for targets. The guns were hand-me-downs from the US Army in Vietnam.

They were unreliable, frequently jammed, and ended up being more about show than defense. The process to get these back into action after jamming would take several minutes while the gunner would potentially be exposed to enemy fire. Since they were mounted on the open handrail, there wasn't any protection, so it was not a desirable place to be while under attack. I was not part of the crew assigned to man the guns. This job was for the deckhands. Whether they were assigned or volunteered I have no idea.

Bored and looking for something to occupy our time while drifting off the coast, we had time to go fishing. We tied a rope to a meat hook, baited with a rancid chunk of meat from the galley, tossed it over the side and tried our luck. Surprisingly, we managed to catch a shark! It was too large for us to pull onboard, but we did manage to pull its head out of the water enough to touch its coarse sandpaper-like skin. The rope was eventually cut to release it into the sea.

Pueblo was finally able to tie up to the Navy dock near downtown San Diego. Sea trials were about to start but I was not involved. Training and testing were for the older and more experienced crewmen who were responsible for the ship's operation. One required test was to see how far Pueblo could roll to starboard or port before it began to capsize. Pueblo's sea trial passed, and they determined it could take a forty-three-degree roll before going past the point of no return. Later in our voyage, while we were passing through a gale, I was told she rolled beyond forty-seven degrees. She struggled, but did manage to right herself before the next big wave. It must be some kind of fudge factor, but that was an eye-popping moment.

Like all liberties in port, money was tight for us lower-ranked swabbies. We spent most of our off-duty time walking around downtown San Diego trying to find cheap places to eat. When leaving ship in any port we had to wear our class-A uniform. Lockers would have to be rented to hold our civies if we wanted to blend in. But the truth is, no swabbie blends in while on shore leave. Civies don't help a bit.

OPEN SEAS TO HAWAII

Departing stateside, little did we know what awaited the next 12 months of our lives. We sailed off to Hawaii with great anticipation for our first exotic port. The thought of going across the ocean to an island paradise seemed inviting, considering the furthest I had ever traveled before enlisting in the Navy was to Colorado. We arrived in Hawaii sailing around the southern end past the Kilauea volcano. Kilauea is a shield volcano located on the big island of Hawaii. Renowned for its consistent volcanic activity, it's one of the most active volcanoes on Earth. I witnessed my first active volcano from afar and it was impressive!

We would spend most of our time on base where everything was less expensive. My fellow band member and friend from home, John Folk, joined the Navy with me. He was already stationed in Hawaii attending radioman school. Whenever we could get together, we enjoyed the sights, paid our respects at the USS Arizona Memorial, walked the streets of Honolulu and strolled the beach at Waikiki.

Many times, we ended up at a club on base where we both were old enough to drink. When time rolled around for Pueblo to get on with her mission, we said our goodbyes near the ship, then he went his way, and I went mine. It would be nearly two years before John and I came into contact with each other again. We did not start another band after returning home but remained longtime friends.

Before leaving for our next port, I wanted to find something to send home to Mom, something special from Hawaii, something different. Mom loved her flowers, so I started shopping at the local florist. The same-day flower-delivery services did not exist in those days, so the problem I thought I had was that a fresh flower would not ship well, especially given the amount of time it would take to arrive in Kansas, some 3,900 miles away.

The florist suggested a live flower that would make the trip. It was boxed up for shipping, and that is what I sent. The flower shop where I purchased the flower assured me it would make it to Kansas. The flower did make it to Kansas alive, and Mom loved it! Soon after, we headed out for Japan, and that would be the last item or letter I would send to her for quite some time.

San Diego was the last time I had the opportunity to call Mom on the phone. I would call her every week while on the mainland, just to let her know what was happening in my life. In turn she would keep me informed on the gossip in Alta Vista, Kansas, and what Mom and Dad were up to. After Hawaii, letters were the only communication I had with my parents.

YOKOSUKA, JAPAN

Whenever we hit port, in the states or overseas, there would always be local civilian workers who would come aboard to fix mechanical problems or install new gear. Pueblo had an ongoing issue with the ship's steering malfunctioning at sea, so this was a frequent issue to be addressed by these civilians.

I do not know how many times it quit working from the time we left Bremerton until arriving in Hawaii, but it was a major concern. When the steering went on the blink, rope and tackle had to be rigged to steer the ship manually. I cannot imagine what would have happened to us if we hit bad weather with malfunctioning steering.

I always thought it seemed odd to have civilian dock workers on-board a US Navy vessel, no matter what port, US or foreign. These Japanese workers in Yokosuka or Sasebo did not act like they understood or spoke English. One guy always seemed happy, smiling all the time and was very courteous to us, but he had an awful craving for sugar. Coffee was always available to anyone who wanted a cup. He would fill his cup with sugar, then add a couple tablespoons of coffee for taste. The cooks finally hid the sugar from him so there would be enough for the rest of us. Yokosuka was the first overseas port where we could relax and spend more time on dry land.

We spent most of our time off in bars drinking, sharing tall tales and wild stories. Several bars were off limits to the military for one reason or another, possibly for being in a rough area I suppose.

Yokosuka, Japan, bar night, l to r: Duane, Mike, Steve, Rich and companion for the night. My favorite photo of my friends was taken at a Yokosuka bar by one of the barmaids. There were usually around four or five of us who hung around together, depending on who had duty that day or night. That night, it was Duane, Mike, Rich and me. Rich is sitting behind the barmaid in this picture. Even though I was the youngest by at least a couple of years we all had a blast being around each other. It was as if we had grown up together doing what friends do on a night out, without girlfriends, well, maybe one. Steven Woelk photo.

We would go to one favorite place where we could take our own bottle but would have to buy the mixer from the bar. The barmaids were friendly and fun to be around. We drank a lot. It's what we did on shore duty to pass through the boredom, but it never seemed to affect our ability to get back to the base.

One weekend, several of us decided we would venture to Yokohama to do some sightseeing. Traveling by train was the most reasonable and fastest mode of transportation readily available. From the train station we found a nearby hotel to stay for the night. An older Japanese lady carried our bags to our rooms. When we tried to tip her, she acted very upset for some reason. We later learned you do not tip in Japan, or at least it was not appropriate then.

We found a cafe nearby where we could experience authentic Japanese food, but the language barrier was a challenge. The innkeeper suggested a place within walking distance. When the menus were handed out, we realized this was not going to be as easy as we thought. The menu had pictures of the food, so we ordered spaghetti. Guess this was the Italian night special.

The following day we took the train to a historical park to see several large Buddha statues. What happened next ended our adventurous outings in Japan.

One night at our favorite watering hole in Yokosuka there were a bunch of us from the ship having a good time. One of my fellow shipmates took a nasty fall while in the head, splitting his skull wide open. An ambulance was called to take him back to the base for treatment. We all stood around the ambulance waiting to regroup to go back inside to finish out the evening.

I lost sight of the rest of the guys when the ambulance took off for the base. When I went back into the bar, I learned that all my friends were gone. They apparently all jumped in the ambulance to hitch a ride back to the base, leaving me to fend for myself. I was all alone wondering how I was going to get back to base.

I was getting a little paranoid, because we usually split cab fares when out and about. But that night caught me with little to nothing in my pockets. I started walking in the pitch dark, following the street I was sure led back to the main gate. It took me about an hour, but I did make it back to the ship before roll call.

Later I was told that Americans in uniform should not venture out on their own, after dark, because some of the locals would cut your throat if given the chance. Luckily it was after midnight when most people were asleep. I never went out again without enough cab fare in my pocket to get back to the base.

Dad told me before I left for the Navy, the guys you associate with, run around with and become friends with will have an impact on what kind of a person you will turn out to be in the future. I made some good friends in the Navy. We were so close, it seemed as if we had hung out together all our lives. I think Dad was proud of how I turned out.

One of our favorite places to visit after a night on the town was a fast-food place called Wimpy's. This joint served hamburgers and fries, but our favorite was their chili. I think it had more hot sauce than tomato sauce, burning your mouth for an hour afterwards. It became our remedy for sobering up.

When we left Yokosuka, Pueblo sailed to Sasebo, Japan, for supplies and more repairs. Steering continued to be problematic. I understood that whenever we docked at a different port along our journey, Pueblo would take receipt of fresh copies of classified documents. This would prove troublesome in the future.

Sasebo was no different than any other port. Like clockwork, on liberty we went to a bar to drink the night away. Drinking was our pastime from duties aboard ship. The booze, beer, and cigarettes were cheap and easy to get on base. I was amazed how much booze was kept in personal lockers on the ship. I never took a drink while on board Pueblo, because I did not want to get caught with a bottle in my possession.

We enjoyed our nights out having fun. If I had continued with that routine, I may have developed a serious drinking problem. The following year in captivity I craved the taste of alcohol more than anything. Thankfully, I did not pick up the habit after I left the Navy.

After resupplying and completing repairs in Sasebo, we left for open seas, sailing toward our first mission. When the seas were rough and we felt adventurous, we would go out on the deck to take in the sea air. On some of the rougher days we would stand next to the exterior handrail watching the water rise above the deck to at least forty feet, then fall below the deck another forty feet, rocking back and forth all the time. The props would come out of the water shaking the entire ship until they settled back down churning towards the next big wave.

When we went through the gale it was seriously rough. I do not know how the old floating hunk of steel made it through, but it did. Everyone was surprised the steering performed and we lost no men overboard.

During the trip, with two swim calls at sea, the ship would stop, drop anchor to allow anyone not on duty to go swimming. I had duty both times, but I probably would not have gone in anyway. There was an accident during one of our swim calls when a crewman jumped off the side of the ship, accidentally falling on another sailor in the water. He was injured enough that he had to be transferred at sea from our ship to a destroyer off to our port side.

We tried to use a boatswain chair strung on a cable between ships, but the sea was too rough. The empty chair spent as much time in the water between ships as it did in the air. So the Captain ordered the ship's lifeboat, also known as the "captain's dinghy," to be launched and transfer the injured sailor around to the destroyer. A Boatswain's Mate navigated the lifeboat to the other ship and back through the pitching waves. He was good at his job, but the transfer with rough seas was challenging, even for him.

I decided to keep practicing my music, so I brought my 1964 Gretsch guitar to the ship when we deployed from Bremerton. A fellow shipmate brought his Gretsch and amplifier so we would jam together as often as we could, to pass the time. If it was a nice day, we would find a corner to play outside on the deck. We very seldom had an audience, and no one seemed to be interested in the type of music we played. Playing our guitars, shooting the bull or just enjoying the calm days at sea was about all we had to do when not on duty.

On board USS Pueblo somewhere in the Pacific Ocean, Steven Woelk on the left, Rich Arnold on right. Steven Woelk photo.

CHAPTER 5
Navy Boot Camp

A s we motored across the endless Pacific Ocean, I often thought back to how I got there.

The night before shipping out for Navy boot camp, a potent cocktail of nerves and excitement bubbled within me. Sleep was out of the question, and the pre-dawn quiet held a strange allure.

There sat our dusty Ford station wagon, a relic from a bygone era. Dad had warned me repeatedly not to touch it—the cracked manifold spewed out an obnoxious racket, transforming the car into a glorified wheeze machine. Yet, the temptation was irresistible. Just a quick spin around town, a final hurrah before the regimented life of the Navy awaited. Convincing myself it was a harmless prank, I slid behind the wheel and ignited the engine.

The racket that erupted shattered the stillness of the night. Dad knew from the noise it could only come from the car he instructed me not to drive. He lept out of bed, threw on some clothes, jumped in our other car and headed my way. He stopped me on my second loop around the half mile stretch of Main Street.

His disappointment stung worse than any lecture. He wasn't just mad about the car; it was the blatant disregard for his instructions, the recklessness that could have jeopardized everything. Shamefaced, I crept back home, the joyride, a distant memory replaced by a crushing sense of reality and regret. He said since I was leaving town in good standing, I should not jeopardize my reputation by being an idiot. My fun was over.

That night was a turning point. It served as a stark reminder of the responsibility that came with adulthood, the importance of respecting boundaries, and the ripple effect of our actions. As I hugged my dad goodbye the next morning, the unspoken apology hung heavily in the air. This wasn't just a farewell; it was a chance to wipe the slate clean, to embark on a new chapter with a newfound respect for his guidance. The cracked manifold became a symbol of my youthful folly, a permanent reminder of the lesson learned on that quiet night before I left for the Navy.

DEPARTING KANSAS CITY TO THE
SAN DIEGO NAVAL TRAINING CENTER

There were three of us, friends from home on the verge of life-changing experiences in the Navy and seeing the Union Station train depot in Kansas City bustling with nervous energy. We joined the throng, three wide-eyed teenagers from small-town Kansas, feeling both apprehensive and strangely exhilarated as we embarked on a pivotal encounter to become Navy men.

Our hotel, nestled in a shadowy corner of downtown, was a far cry from the comfort of home. Dimly lit hallways and heavily trafficked carpets hinted at a history best left unexplored. The air crackled with a tension that wasn't entirely unwelcome—a sense of adventure tinged with the ever-present awareness of being far from familiar territory.

Like most teenagers on the prowl far from home, we were ready to hit the streets. Although the "ladies of the night" were noticeably present, our focus turned to something else. The thought of propositioning may have been on our minds, but our billfolds were not fat enough to pursue those lustful interests. The streets, slick with grime and poorly lit, seemed to stretch on endlessly.

We encountered multiple groups of men huddled in doorways, speaking in hushed conversations punctuated by bursts of laughter. We steered clear, our youthful faces betraying our naiveté. We needed something to ease the jitters and calm the nerves—BEER.

Our initial plan—cross the state line into Kansas, the mythical land of 18-year-old drinking privileges—proved embarrassingly misguided. After hours of aimlessly wandering, we stumbled upon a dingy liquor store, a beacon of hope in the urban night.

With a mix of bravado and trepidation, we entered, half expecting a stern rebuke. Instead, the cashier, a wizened man with a perpetual smirk, simply rang up our purchase—a six-pack of our favorite beer. Jubilant at our unexpected success, we retreated to the sanctuary of our hotel room. Sharing one last drink served its purpose among friends on the cusp of a new chapter of life. Tasting freedom, somewhat rebellious and with a bittersweet pang of leaving childhood behind, we were ready to take the next step.

SAN DIEGO

After processing through the Union Station recruit intake facility, we boarded our train for Navy boot camp in San Diego. There were other recruits headed for the Naval Training Center (NTC) in San Diego, which was ultimately closed because of sweeping base closures following the end of the Cold War in 1993.

The rattling train ride to San Diego was a monotonous blur of endless tracks and rolling hills. Yet, amidst the boredom, a sense of camaraderie began to blossom. We swapped stories, anxieties and dreams, forging a tentative bond with other young men who would become our brothers-in-arms.

One recruit, a wisecracking Kansas City native named Joey, regaled us with tales of his street smarts, a stark contrast to my sheltered small-town upbringing. Another, a lanky farm boy from Paola, Kansas, possessed an uncanny ability to sleep through anything, even the conductor's periodic bellow. Hours went by as we'd steal away a random power nap, staring out the window or observing other occupants of the rail car. These snippets of life, shared in the confines of the train car, painted a human portrait of the diverse group of soon to be swabbies.

Boot camp was a whirlwind of activity, a relentless assault on our bodies and minds. Drill Instructors (DIs) with booming voices and perpetually furrowed brows, reveled in transforming us from civilians into sailors. We marched until our legs ached, drilled until our movements became second nature, and policed each other's every misstep. Despite the physical and mental strain, a bond of camaraderie grew among us. We shared inside jokes, offered words of encouragement, and celebrated each other's small victories.

One particularly grueling day of marching on the grinder led to solace huddled together under the thin blanket of night, sharing stories from home and dreams of the future. Laughter, albeit strained, filled the air, a testament to the resilience of the human spirit. Smoking, courtesy of the DI barking, "The smoking lamp is now lit," was a newly accepted way of life, no more watching over our shoulders for someone to scold us about sneaking a smoke. My memory of boot camp is that everyone smoked. Even the first timers, wanting to fit in with the crowd.

KP duty was introduced as a dreaded but necessary task. The sheer volume of food preparation was mind-boggling. Mountains of potatoes awaited peeling, vats of bubbling liquid transformed into something vaguely resembling soup, and endless trays of glistening bacon emerged from colossal steam ovens. KP came and went with the appreciation for those men and women who rattled pots and pans for a living.

Food service would not be for me.

One particularly chaotic afternoon, I found myself assigned to the dishwashing pit. Armed with a rubber apron and a burning desire to avoid reprimands, I attacked the mountain of greasy trays with fervent zeal. However, my enthusiasm was misplaced. In my haste, I managed to send a tray of silverware clattering to the floor, earning a withering look from the grizzled KP duty chief. Boot camp, it seemed, offered endless opportunities to learn both about myself and the intricacies of large-scale dishwashing.

The white hat or "dixie cup," a symbol of naval pride, became an ongoing source of frustration. Night after night, I would meticulously scrub the wide band, rinsing it repeatedly to ensure its pristine whiteness. It took some time to accomplish the proper procedure in getting that hat white, but I managed to succeed. The stubborn fabric seemed to hold onto the faintest traces of soap, leaving a telltale yellow ring that no amount of scrubbing could erase.

My fellow recruits, some veritable shoe-shining virtuosos, offered countless pointers, but their techniques only served to worsen the problem. This seemingly trivial struggle became a metaphor for my boot camp experience—a constant battle against limitations, a yearning for perfection that was ultimately unattainable. Yet, amidst the frustration, a newfound appreciation for perseverance began to take root. Perhaps, I mused, a dull shine was better than none at all.

The looming shadow of the swimming qualification test cast a dark cloud over our days. I passed, being able to go the distance, tread water and make a floatation device out of my dungarees, but it was a struggle. While some recruits glided effortlessly through the water, I resembled a panicked puppy attempting to doggy paddle. I never was a great swimmer but always felt I would be able to save myself in case of an emergency.

The prospect of jumping off a tower supposedly mimicking the lowest level of an aircraft carrier deck filled me with dread. My heart hammered against my ribs as we shuffled toward the base of the structure, the platform looming high above us, each step a testament to my mounting terror. Just as I reached the bottom of the stairs, bracing myself for the ascent, a barked command sent a jolt through the line. Apparently, an urgent "adventure" awaited us, sparing the last group of us from the watery ordeal (at least for now).

Vaccinations became a dreaded ritual, a periodic punctuation to our already rigorous routine. The sight of the corpsman walking toward us with his tray of high-pressure air guns filled some with apprehension, but accepting it was a necessary part of training in preparation for what might be in store for us in the future. The hissing penetration of the liquid left behind a fleeting sting, others a dull ache that lingered for days.

The corpsman cautioned us, "If you move the slightest bit, this pressurized spray could leave a nasty gash in your upper arm." The most dreaded shot was the one administered to the thigh. It would immediately start to seize the thigh muscle with extreme pain. The best way to counter this temporary discomfort was to march it off. For some unknown reason I did not have to take this injection in the thigh. Not sure if it was because I am allergic to penicillin or something else, but I did not argue and was good with that.

Bilge fire training was a unique experience for everyone in my group. It was obvious none of us had any previous training on how to fight this type of fire. After some preliminary instruction it was time to man the hoses. We were ushered into a large, steel enclosure, the air thick with anticipation and the faint scent of oil.

A fiery inferno erupted on the water's surface, mimicking a blaze raging beneath the expanded metal decks above a ship's bilge. The instructors barked instructions, herding us toward the fire ahead. The sweet spot was at the nozzle, a constant stream of water providing a precious pocket of breathable air amidst the smoke and heat. A snorkel on a nozzle provided cool water from overhead showering down on us all decked out in our firefighting gear.

We battled the flames, inch by agonizing inch, pushing them back into the corners of the simulated bilge. Elated by our near victory, we momentarily forgot the ever-present danger. The fire, a cunning adversary, had crept behind us, silently blocking our escape route. Just as panic threatened to engulf us, the instructors yanked us out, their gruff voices laced with a hint of satisfaction. The training may have been abruptly terminated, but the lesson remained etched in our minds: complacency could be just as deadly as fire itself.

The gas chamber was a different kind of beast altogether. Marched in, gas masks strapped on, we resembled a grotesque parade of faceless entities. The initial sensation was one of suffocating tightness, the mask's rubber seal clinging to my face with an almost obscene intimacy. A false sense of security settled in as we adjusted the filters, the world reduced to a muffled quiet.

Then, with a hiss, the gas was released. Within the chamber the dreaded order came, "Take off your masks." A searing pain erupted in my eyes, a tidal wave of discomfort that ripped through my entire body. Instinct took over, hands scrambling to pull the mask back on, gasping for precious clean air. Around me, coughs and choked gasps filled the air, a symphony of human misery. The ordeal, thankfully, was short-lived, but the burning aftereffects in my lungs lingered, a potent reminder of the horrors chemical warfare could unleash.

The aptitude tests proved to be a psychological hurdle with the potential to shape my future. While some approached them with nonchalance, I couldn't help but feel a gnawing anxiety. Did I possess the skills the Navy sought? Was I destined for a life of scrubbing decks or could I aspire for something more? The tests themselves were a blur of questions, logic puzzles, and mechanical contraptions. Emerging from the final exam, I felt a strange mix of relief and apprehension. The results would be a mystery until later, leaving me to speculate on the path that awaited me.

Boot camp forged an unlikely bond between my two high school buddies and me. We were three peas in a pod, navigating the uncharted waters of military life together. One evening, while sharing a pack of cigarettes, we found ourselves discussing the upcoming Christmas break.

The dilemma was stark: two weeks of leave now, forfeiting the post-boot camp vacation, or stay put and celebrate a subdued Christmas with limited duty. Home, with its familiar comforts and loving families, beckoned many of us with undeniable allure. Yet, the thought of missing out on the camaraderie of our final weeks together felt equally daunting.

After much deliberation, and fueled by whispered conversations with a shared longing, we made our decision. We would forgo the immediate gratification of home, choosing instead to spend Christmas with our newfound Navy family, a testament to the bond forged in the crucible of boot camp.

The grinder, usually a relentless symbol of drill instructor-induced misery, transformed into a stage for our grand finale. A sea of dress blue uniforms, pristine white leggings and belts, gleaming shoes, and shouldered rifles stretched as far as the eye could see, a testament to the weeks of relentless drilling and scrubbing. A nervous energy crackled through the ranks, punctuated by hushed conversations and the occasional burst of laughter. Amidst the throng, I spotted my two buddies, their faces mirroring my own mix of excitement and apprehension. We exchanged a quick grin, a silent reassurance in the face of the imminent ceremony.

Donning the dress uniform for the first time was a revelation. Navy dress blues felt foreign yet strangely comforting, a physical manifestation of the transformation we had undergone. Standing ramrod straight, I marveled at the sharp reflection staring back at me in the barracks window.

Was this still the pudgy-cheeked kid who had arrived at boot camp weeks ago? A pang of nostalgia tugged at me, a bittersweet reminder of the life I had left behind. Just then, a mischievous glint appeared in my friend's eye. He pointed to a white splatter adorning my pristine trousers—a rogue dab of toothpaste from a morning

San Diego boot camp in dress blues, l to r: John Folk, Steven Woelk, Scotty McDiffett. Steven Woelk photo.

mishap. A wave of laughter washed over us, a brief reprieve from the weight of the ceremony.

The arrival of my parents sent a jolt of pure joy through me. Their faces, etched with a mixture of pride and relief, were a welcome beacon in the sea of unfamiliar faces. Later, during a stolen moment amidst the post-ceremony chaos, my mom dabbed at a stray tear, whispering how proud she was of the young man I had become.

The uniform, once a symbol of discipline and hardship, now represented a new chapter, a future filled with both uncertainty and the unwavering support of my family. My three buddies and I had another surprise waiting for us after graduation. A fellow female schoolmate from Alta Vista High School was there to congratulate us. Evelyn had joined the Navy and graduated earlier than the rest of us. My parents, friends and her all went out for lunch together.

Fifty-one of us graduated in Company 598 on that day. After boot camp, the three of us took our two weeks leave to go home. After landing in Kansas City, we took a commuter plane to Manhattan, Kansas. After wrangling a ride downtown, we called a friend back home to pick us up and bring us back to Alta Vista.

When I was home on leave, I did not have a girlfriend nor was I particularly looking for anyone to start a new relationship. A couple of close high school friends introduced me to a girl they met while attending college in Emporia. She lived in Burns, just outside of Eldorado. We went out a couple of times while I was home but she lived two hours away so it was difficult to establish any type of meaningful relationship in just two weeks. We exchanged a few letters but the Pueblo Incident put a stop to that romantic story.

CHAPTER 6
General Quarters! All Hands on Deck

A General Quarters (GQ) drill is a serious event on a Navy ship, signaling practice for a potential threat or emergency. When the alarm sounds, every crew member must quickly move to their assigned battle station. What happens during a GQ drill?

Distinctive alarm blasts, often a loud klaxon or general alarm, are sounded throughout the ship. It is unmistakable and cannot be ignored, no matter where you are on the ship. All sailors and officers rush to their assigned battle stations, which could be anywhere from the bridge to the engine room. Once at their stations, all crew members assume their assigned roles, which include:

- Damage Control: Repairing damage to the ship.
- Fire Fighting: Extinguishing fires.
- Combat Systems: Operating weapons systems and sensors.
- Navigation: Steering the ship and avoiding threats.
- Medical Services: Treating the wounded.

The drill is conducted under the supervision of officers, and the crew's performance is evaluated. After the drill, the crew gathers for a debriefing to discuss lessons learned and identify areas for improvement. The purpose of GQ drills is to train the crew to respond quickly and effectively to a variety of threats, from enemy attacks to natural disasters. By practicing these drills regularly, the Navy ensures that its ships are prepared to handle any challenge.

Little did we know just how important this drill would be in the future.

THE SEA OF JAPAN

Bucher writes about his friend, Lieutenant Commander Charles Clark, another surfaced submariner like himself, promising to keep him informed about his experiences on the Banner. A series of vivid letters to Bucher mentioned furious storms, dangerous icing on his superstructure, and Russian patrol boats coming at him with guns manned and signal flags warning: HEAVE TO OR I WILL FIRE. In an odd set of circumstances, while the Chinese and Russians would send out combat ships in efforts to intimidate Banner, the North Koreans hadn't reacted on the two occasions when the Banner passed by their coast. This takes us back to fallout from the "Blue House Incident." The North Koreans would hedge their bets and play a dangerous game of chess.

THE CONFRONTATION

We had been at sea for most of January, somewhere off the coast of a country I knew nothing about at the time. For reasons I didn't understand, we would remain in one location for a time, bobbing up and down or moving further away from the coast. While taking soundings off the main deck as part of my regular watch duties on 22 January, I saw a fishing trawler some distance off on the horizon but thought nothing of it. We had seen fishing trawlers before and there was never any reason to get alarmed about it.

The following day was freezing cold, with calm seas. Around noon, crew members began to observe as many as five warships heading in our direction. Two Russian MiGs would soon join the pursuit as they all approached Pueblo at great speed. The first ship coming within a close distance flew a red and blue striped flag with a red star on a white background. I had no idea what country the flag represented but would soon find out. From the pilot house, Captain Bucher saw us gazing out the hatch and ordered us back inside. I stepped back inside and secured the hatch, but I could see soldiers standing on the deck of one of the ships closest to us, AK-47s in the ready position with fingers on the triggers, all focused intently on Pueblo. The scuttlebutt around the ship affirmed for everyone that we were sitting in international waters, off the coast of North Korea.

The Democratic People's Republic of Korea (DPRK) gun boats put up signal flags ordering Pueblo to prepare for a boarding party. Captain Bucher answered back that we were a United States Navy vessel operating in international waters. We ignored their request to board by trying to move away at a flank speed of 15 knots.

The General Quarters alarm sounded when it was determined we had a serious situation brewing. I had already moved to the forward berthing area before GQ sounded.

To my surprise, I noticed water sloshing on the floor toward the back bulkhead close to where my bunk was located. Coincidentally, this was where I stored my guitar. I did not have time to do anything about it, but I imagine sea water on guitars is not a good thing. That would be the last time I saw my Gretsch.

I left the berthing quarters and headed to the Auxiliary Engine Room, my GQ station. Duane Hodges was already in the engine room on the ship's communications system. He and I were the only two assigned to this space during General Quarters. Each crew member had his own GQ assignment. Some wore the ship's internal communication headsets, some were assigned to specific equipment necessary for the operation of critical systems. My duty was to stand watch on the water purifying evaporator in the Auxiliary Engine Room.

MACHINE GUNS AGAINST MIGS & GUNBOATS

We started hearing gunfire and it was difficult to carry on a conversation with the loud noise coming from the generator running at full capacity. But we could hear the faint plinking sound of something hitting the bulkhead. The chaos was just beginning.

We had no idea Pueblo was being torn apart by 57-mm cannon shells, heavy and light machine-gun fire coming from all directions, and MiGs roaring overhead while strafing the water around us. The North Koreans took aim at the pilot house, trying to disable the ship's control.

Everyone who was in the pilot house was hit with either shrapnel or flying glass from the attack. It wasn't long until Duane was ordered up to the main deck, where he was told to help in the destruction of Top Secret and classified materials. Soon after Duane left, I was ordered up to the same area where he was located. When I

USS Pueblo under attack by North Korean Navy gunboats and MiG combat aircraft on January 23, 1968, while motoring 16 miles off the coast of North Korea, in international waters. Painting by Richard DeRosset.

arrived, Duane was crouching with Charlie Crandall and Bob Chicca in a short passageway along an exterior bulkhead, midships, starboard side.

There was not enough room for all four of us, so I was positioned in a connecting passageway. My new assignment was to remove all the contents from an already opened safe containing Top Secret documents located near Captain Bucher's berthing quarters. I knew that Bob Hill was also in the same passageway as the other three, but I was unable to see him.

Top side, Captain Bucher was stalling for time by avoiding the North Koreans as much as possible while under fire. Hopelessly outgunned, his plan was to hold out long enough to allow the US Navy time to come to our rescue, or at the very least respond to the aggression of the North Koreans.

The CTs broke radio silence and communicated with the Navy about our situation, desperately demanding assistance. The Pueblo had not been equipped with enough firepower to fend off such an overwhelming attack. The two 50-caliber machine guns would be futile and useless in this battle, even if the gunners managed to avoid getting hit while loading the guns and powering them up. They would have had to haul multiple magazines of 50-caliber shells across twenty feet of open deck, climb up an eight-foot ladder while exposed to a hail of bullets coming in from all sides by enemy gunboats at close range. They never would have made it. At the time of the attack, one machine gun was mounted on the forecastle, covered with canvas and ice. The second machine gun was stored aft, below deck.

Back at my position, I started removing everything from inside the safe, handing its contents to Bob Chicca. He tore up the documents, put them into a trash can where a fire was already burning. The government-issued metal trash cans were a very inefficient way

Looking out the hatch where Duane, Bob and Charlie were located during the attack by North Korean Navy. North Korean Navy photo.

to dispose of mounds of documents and manuals, but that is all the Navy gave us. There was a small incinerator for the CTs' use, but it was too small for the volume they had to destroy.

Duane, Charlie, and Bob Hill were receiving the same type of material from another passageway hatch leading toward the SOD HUT. There were several locations around the interior of the ship where crew members were burning documents as well. The smoke was unbearable throughout the interior of the ship, making it difficult for anyone to see or breathe. To clear the smoke from our area, Bob Chicca opened an exterior hatch so at least some of the smoke would clear.

The hatch opened toward the stern of the ship, so no one from the starboard side or the back of Pueblo could see us. They could see the smoke coming out of the hatch but could not see what we were doing. The view from nearby ships was blocked by a solid metal exterior handrail less than four feet high.

The gunfire was increasing from all directions as the North Koreans attempted to disable the ship or at least eliminate the crew trying to keep control. We could hear the bullets pinging against the hull and ripping into the sides of Pueblo.

I happened to be facing Bob Chicca from about five feet when the blast occurred.

I remember hearing a loud explosion, smelling the pungent odor of gunpowder burning through steel which added to the already smoky passageway.

SHRAPNEL BLAST

A 57-mm shell hit midship starboard side about five feet above the water line, right where Duane, Charlie and Bob Chicca were positioned. Bob Hill was knocked off his feet by the blast concussion and lay unconscious on the deck until help arrived to pull him out of

Gun locker riddled with bullet holes near Duane's, Bob's and Charlie's position. Caption for the second photo: Antenna base hit with a .57mm shell. North Korean Navy photos.

the area. He did not receive any shrapnel from the blast. The shrapnel blast hit the other three crouched on the deck.

Small fragments of shrapnel from the same blast came down the passageway striking me while I was kneeling toward the explosion. The shrapnel and the intense heat from the blast knocked me over backwards. I felt an extremely dull pain in my crotch and a burning sensation on my chest and lip where small pieces of shrapnel hit my upper body. I lay there flat on my back in shock, not realizing what had just happened.

Foot traffic was picking up in this very narrow, short passageway. Everyone was rushing toward Duane, Bob and Charlie while stepping over me and stumbling down the passageway. No one seemed to be concerned about me lying motionless, bleeding profusely on the deck and blocking half the passageway.

Wanting to get out of the way, I noticed that the officer's mess was around the corner, so I pulled myself on my back a short distance through the open door with a trail of blood behind me. I could not move from the waist down without extreme pain. I was on my side with my head pointing starboard, feet to port, between the dining table, countertop and serving cabinets. I knew I was wounded in the groin but had no idea how severely. My dungarees, soaked with blood, were ripped wide open in the crotch. I could hardly move but knew I needed medical help soon.

There was so much chaos, alarms sounding, men yelling, explosions rocking the boat and sailors rushing in every conceivable direction. Some tended the wounded, others raced to their General Quarters positions, and all tried to carry out orders from the officers and Chief Petty Officers.

All this chaos was happening around me but in my shocked and wounded state, I was unable to do anything about it.

I had no idea what happened to Duane, Charlie, or Bob Chicca. They were all in the area where a huge explosion occurred. It got worse, as all hell soon broke loose.

Not until the next day did I learn that Charlie Crandell suffered a severe burn and shrapnel in his leg from the fireball of the blast. Bob Chicca had a piece of shrapnel embedded high on his inner thigh just missing his femoral artery and grazing his scrotum. Duane Hodges must have been right where the 57-mm exploded as his wounds were extensive across his waist.

Our ship's corpsman, "Doc" Baldridge, was unable to provide any assistance due to Duane's extensive wounds in his hip and groin. If Duane's wounds were as bad as Doc explained to me much later, my best friend would not have lasted more than a minute or two.

Shortly after the blast, Duane was put into a wire stretcher and carried to the passageway outside the officers' mess door. Doc positioned himself between Duane and me, trying desperately to save Duane.

Doc also applied field bandages on my injuries, trying to stop the bleeding. He administered at least one syrette of morphine to ease my pain. Doc told me later the only thing that kept me from bleeding to death was the pressure from lying on my bandages. The morphine worked fine if I didn't move my legs, but it did not last long.

I was in a lot of pain when I moved from the waist down. I was in a good mood, no doubt from the morphine or maybe it was because I truly believed I would soon be in a Navy hospital being tended to properly.

Officer's mess dining table where Steven Woelk lay, severely wounded. North Korean Navy photo.

It was obvious that Pueblo had been attacked, we were unable to defend our ship and would soon be seized by that crushing enemy force.

When the North Koreans grabbed control of Pueblo, armed soldiers began to appear on deck, walking back and forth, hollering in a language unfamiliar to me, and peaking inside where I was located. I was unaware at what point Duane's body had been removed from the passageway.

Before Doc was forcefully taken away, I was placed on top of the officer's dining table on the plastic cover. As they escorted Doc away, a North Korean soldier was ordered to stand beside me, as if I was going to run away. One of the first things he did was to take my wristwatch. I was wearing my high school class ring, but he was not interested in it for some reason, and I was allowed to keep the ring throughout my entire captivity.

The North Korean guards seemed to be more interested in taking trinkets like watches, rings, and personal items rather than focusing on the treasure trove of classified documents and equipment they had just seized.

The commotion up and down the passageway was still very intense and continued for quite some time. When the noise began to quiet down, a North Korean officer stepped through the door every now and then, saying something to the guard, then leaving. Everything was settling down outside the officers' mess, and all I remember hearing was the roar of the main engines down the passageway. The doors to the engine room must have been open, drowning out the sounds from what was going on up front.

I do not have any idea how long I lay on the table before the North Koreans started to direct their attention toward me. Two guards bound my hands, tied my ankles together, blindfolded me, wrapped me in the plastic table cover, threw a blanket over me. They pulled me off the table and with a thud, I landed on the deck, then they dragged me down the passageway. My wish of being rescued by the Navy was fading fast.

I had no idea where we were, or where we were going. I just assumed we were still at sea. Without seeing anything from under my blindfold, I feared they were about to toss me in the ocean. It is amazing how many thoughts cross your stressed-out mind in such situations when you fear the worst.

If I was thrown overboard, I would not be able to swim in my condition. The water was extremely cold, nighttime darkness enveloped us, and the surrounding air temperatures were freezing. At least I would not have suffered very long in the water. When I heard the guard in front step onto the ship's aluminum gangplank, I felt certain I would not be tossed into the water.

The guards lifted me up just enough so they could drag me onto shore. From there they continued dragging me on the ground to a bus where I was placed between the seats. My blindfold had loosened somewhat so I could see many of the crew were already on this bus bound and blindfolded as well.

Between the time we docked and I was taken from the ship, the crew was assembled outside, up front, bound and blindfolded, sitting on the cold deck, in subfreezing weather. Many wore only shirts, but a few were able to get to their heavier coats.

The USS Pueblo remains the only commissioned ship held captive by a foreign power.

North Korea has since turned the ship into a museum piece, putting it on display in Pyongyang.

CHAPTER 7
Becoming Prisoners of War

Propaganda photo showing CO Bucher, officers and crew being paraded down a street surrounded by an angry crowd. North Korean Navy photo.

When the crew was taken from Pueblo, they were paraded in single file through a large crowd of North Koreans where they were kicked, slapped, slugged, and spit on. While this was taking place, Korean photographers were already at work snapping propaganda photos.

I was the last crewman to leave the USS Pueblo at Wonsan Harbor. When I was placed on the bus with the rest of my shipmates, the bus drove off. I remember being loaded onto the bus, but I have no recollection of anything else until the bus stopped and we were loaded onto a train.

At some point, they placed me on a stretcher. The seats on the train were wooden benches facing each other in a row on both sides of the train car. My blindfold was now loose enough to see the back of the heads of my fellow crewmen on the bench in front of me. They placed me in a seat near the back of the car. I saw guards walking by or occasionally stopping in the aisle beside me.

While I was still lying uncomfortably in the plastic table covering, they positioned my stretcher across two benches. If it were not for the plastic table cover keeping pressure on my bandages, their dragging me across the ground would have certainly reopened my wounds and caused excessive bleeding.

The crew was apparently sitting in the same type of seats ahead of me but I could not see their faces. The guards covered me in a blanket, but it was so cold, one blanket was by no means enough to warm me up from the freezing temperatures inside that train car.

The throbbing pain from my wounds was intensifying, whether I moved or not. The bleeding had apparently quit from the weight of my body lying on the bandages and I was getting extremely thirsty, so I started pleading for water. The North Korean guards ignored me, but one crewman hollered out to give me some water. I heard a thud, then a moan. One guard slammed his rifle butt against his head to shut him up. I nor anyone else said another word from then on. My thirst would have to linger a while longer.

When the train stopped, all of us were taken off and placed into a dark, cold, filthy building. They put me in the room with Charlie and Bob. We had all been wounded by the same blast. The fourth crew member with us was Dale Rigby, who would turn out to be our guardian angel.

Dale was evidently placed in our room to take care of us. Doc Baldridge would never be allowed to tend to us again. Dale had no medical training other than first aid he learned in Boy Scouts. The

North Koreans provided no medical assistance, bandages, pain relief or help whatsoever. Thank God, He gave us Dale!

I owe Dale, Bob, and Charlie for getting me through that first week of hell.

We were soon moved from one hell hole to another. Just as before, the wounded were put into a room together and Dale remained with us. The stress on Dale had to be tremendous. Day three dawned with no medical help from the North Koreans.

The overpowering stench in our room from the infections, decaying flesh and body fluids was enough to make us sick on top of our open wounds. The guards would wrap bandanas around their face to mask the odor when they entered the room.

After a while they would not come into our room but would instead stick their head in the door like a bully to swear at us, then leave. The Korean word for "Son of a Dog" sounded like "ksuckie," and we were called "sons of dogs" a lot. It was not unlike our use of the term, "son of a bitch."

The food we were served was unrecognizable at times. I remember the first bowl of watered-down soup had some chunky substance that did not look like anything I had ever seen before.

It turns out it was the pig-fat soup I described earlier. They also gave us soup containing cabbage and turnips, and rice was served on the side with every meal. When we mixed rice in with the pig-fat soup, it was edible, but not very nutritional.

It felt as though we were in limbo, with the North Koreans not knowing what to do with us. We wondered if they were preparing for the United States to retaliate, or would the US meet their demands. We also wondered if they were planning a mass execution. They fed us enough to survive, but they did not give us any medical treatment early on.

The water provided to us was boiled to get rid of whatever lingered in their water supply. I learned later that unboiled water caused dysentery almost immediately. Rooms were supplied with one teapot and a single cup for each of us.

The captives in each room were required to ration water evenly between each other. We barely had enough water to sustain life. Late one night, while everyone in my room was asleep, I was so thirsty I drank more than my share of water. I felt bad about it, but I do not believe I was in my right mind. I was delirious and fell in and out of consciousness most of the time.

If I did not receive medical treatment soon, I was going to be the second crewman to die. Dale, Bob, and Charlie were able to convince a North Korean officer that the wounded needed to have more water, and from then on, we received two teapots of water each day.

Ten days passed before they started to medically treat any of the wounded. Other than Bob, Charlie and me, we had no idea who else had been wounded or to what extent, as we weren't allowed to talk or interact with our crewmates. As it turned out, other than Duane, I was the most critically wounded during the attack. Bob was next with the shrapnel in his inner thigh, and then Charlie had burns and bits of shrapnel up the side of his leg.

There were numerous crewmen wounded, but the three of us, as well as Captain Bucher, needed a doctor's care. Apparently, Captain Bucher had a piece of shrapnel in his backside.

SURGERY AND HOSPITAL

Late one night, a couple of guards stomped into our room, bundled me up in the plastic covering from the ward room, and down the hallway we went. My first thought was, dang, they're moving us again. Instead, I alone was taken to a small room a short distance down the hallway.

The room appeared to be either a small kitchen or a medical examination room. It contained a countertop, a table and cabinets on two walls. A single light bulb hung from the ceiling. The guards put me on the table in the center of the room, then tied my hands and feet down so I couldn't move. I thought, "This isn't good."

There were several people in the room. There was a doctor and a couple of nurses, all dressed in white, with masks over their mouths. Of course, there were the ever-present guards. The plastic table cover was finally removed as well as my clothes. As the nurses and guards held me down, they started removing bone fragments from my groin, cutting away the infection and shrapnel without any anesthetic or anything to deaden the pain. What I remember most was the scissors snipping away the infected tissue. Every cut was excruciating. The only way I could withstand the pain was to holler as loudly as I could.

I later found out some of the crew who heard me hollering thought I was being tortured. I was, but not in the way they thought about it! The pain I experienced during my surgery could have been reduced or eliminated by local anesthesia. Such drugs had been in use long before the Pueblo Incident, but for whatever reason, they chose not to use them.

I could not determine how much shrapnel I had in my groin prior to being operated on. Before getting moved into the operating room, I knew there may have been something sharp poking me, whenever I would move my legs. The shrapnel that passed through me couldn't have been much larger than one half inch. One piece of shrapnel hit me in the chest, burning through my shirt, and the piece hitting my lip did not penetrate the skin. They were hot enough to stick and scar but could be easily pulled off. The piece striking my lip was hot enough to burn flesh and burned my tongue like pepper.

I incurred a fractured pelvis involving my right pubic bone and half of my tailbone was blown away. Both of my testicles were damaged to the extent they were surgically removed. They sutured me with what appeared to be a heavy kite string, or the white string used to wrap pieces of meat from the supermarket. Any of the medical procedures they performed on me were void of anesthetic so there was no deadening of the pain.

When they carried me back to the room, they took one of the other wounded sailors to the torture table and operated on him. We were all dealt with in a comparable manner. When they laid me back down in the bed in my room, I was out for the night from shear exhaustion.

Four days later, I had not shown any signs of improvement. If they did not take better care of me, I would be the second fatality. Once again, two guards came into the room at night, bound my hands and feet, covered me with a blanket, blindfolded me and carried me out of the building. They put me in the back of a military jeep and drove off to a North Korean hospital.

This hospital admission would be the second time in my life. During the early to mid-1950s as the polio epidemic spread across the United States, at least five cases were reported in and around the Alta Vista community. I contracted that dreaded disease and was one of those statistics. I made it through the illness to live a normal life with minimal side effects, only to find my adult-self on an operating table in a North Korean hospital. Similarly frightening but in vastly different circumstances.

On the way to this military hospital, I could tell we were on a gravel road. We stopped once upon being approached by a soldier in uniform who was handed papers by my chauffeur. I assume it was authorization to be out late at night. I could see a little light from the edges of my blindfold.

I do remember the sky was clear, full of bright stars and very cold. When we got to our destination, they took me out of the jeep, still on the stretcher, carried me up a flight of stairs, down a hallway and to my new resting place in a secluded room. I was transferred to a wooden frame bed with a hard mattress. Replacing my clothes, they dressed me in hospital attire.

The room was about 10 feet x 15 feet with one dim light bulb hanging from the ceiling. Paint was peeling from the walls and ceiling. The room had a cast iron steam register, straight chair for the doctor to use, small table, teapot with cup, double-hung window with the bottom half painted over. I could not see out the window.

There was also an open transom window over the door. Although the door was closed, I could hear voices in the distance because the transom window above the door was always left open. The floor appeared to be made from very old wood. It was dirty with quarter-inch spaces between each board. Dim lights, dirty floors and walls were

Woelk with his North Korean doctor during a propaganda photo shoot. North Korean propaganda photo.

not what you would expect in a hospital, but this nightmare took place in the hermit kingdom.

The women who brought my food were not wearing uniforms, so I assumed they were not military but hospital cooks. The doctor, nurses, interpreter, and camera crews were all in military attire.

My doctor was nice; he more than likely saved my life, assuming he was the doctor who performed surgery on me in the other building. He always was smiling under his mask when he came around on his daily visits. The nurses only came in to assist the doctor or to give me injections. The interpreter was nice. I later found out the crew named him "Fetch."

I am not sure how they came up with the name. I do not believe I ever witnessed him getting upset with any of us, but he would criticize the United States regularly, calling us, "Imperial aggressors against the DPRK." Only two of the North Koreans who dealt with us were pleasant, my doctor and Fetch. Ship's Corpsman Baldridge told me years after our return home that he would invite the doctor who cared for us into his home anytime. Coming from Doc Baldridge, this really took me by surprise.

How I coped in solitary confinement in the hospital is beyond me. My mind is blank trying to recall the forty-four days of solitude. I did wear out the deck of cards they gave me, playing solitaire. Then there were the magazines they thought I would enjoy reading. Stories about how great their glorious leader is, how advanced they are over anyone else in the world, the strength of their military, and how they would defeat the imperial aggressors with one mighty blow, including pictures depicting US Army MPs or Americans being killed by their army.

I received as many as five injections of a clear liquid per day. I have no idea what was in the clear glass vial, but it did not numb the pain.

FIRST INJURY

Lying in that bed for days on end gave me lots of time to daydream. I thought about my days playing on and near the railroad tracks in Alta Vista. The Rock Island railroad ran within a quarter-mile of my house. It was our portal to the wilderness. We walked many miles up and down those tracks in our younger days. Usually no more than five miles in either direction. There was always a side excursion or distraction that had to be investigated that shortened our journey.

We never had any close calls with trains coming from either direction. Back then, the Rock Island had a busy route on a two-track system. One day I had a chance to ask an engineer while the train was stopped, why the trains struggled through this stretch of track. He told me the 70-plus mile route from Topeka to Harrington, Kansas, was one of the longest incline routes in the U.S.

It's hard to believe, but us kids would fall for any neat story like that. When the trains were going east to west you could hear the engines miles away, especially when they were loaded with the summer wheat harvest. When the engines were unable to make the grade, they would bring another engine out of Topeka to push them up the hill. Running from west to east it was hard to hear them coming, they would fly going downhill loaded or not. We would always walk on the opposite track just in case one would slip up from behind.

Looking back on it now, I think about a quote from the movie *Stand By Me*. It takes place in a final scene but during the present day, years after the events of the film. He reflected on his childhood and the profound impact that his friends and their shared experiences had on his life. He ends his story with, "I never had any friends later on like the ones I had when I was twelve."

My daydreams never lasted long, because of the constant threat of brutal medical treatment.

My fear of needles started at an early age in the emergency room of the local hospital in Council Grove, Kansas.

Trash day always held a certain morbid fascination for me. The towering fifty-five-gallon steel barrel stood sentinel in the backyard, a rusty testament to countless meals and household discards. The air one night was thick with the acrid scent of burning paper and wood. That was a smell that somehow signaled the end of something old and the start of something new.

As I grabbed a hefty bag of trash to throw in the barrel, a sense of foreboding washed over me. The jagged shard of glass seemed to appear out of nowhere. One minute I was heaving the bag into the steel barrel and the next I was doubled over with a scream erupting from my throat.

A searing pain shot through my foot that instantly brought tears to my eyes. Looking down, I saw the culprit—a two-inch sliver of glass protruding from my tennis shoe, like a grotesque trophy. Blood welled up, staining the formerly white canvas with a bright color of crimson.

Panic turned to relief when Bert, our neighbor and ever-dependable scoutmaster, appeared at the back door. His calm demeanor and practical first-aid skills were a godsend. He stemmed the bleeding with a steady hand, loaded me into his car, then sped off to the hospital with me in a blur of pain and anxiety.

The sterile environment of the hospital brought a different kind of ordeal. Our family doctor was a soft-spoken man who was respected by all he treated. The total number of stitches was fourteen, seven inside and seven outside, needed to close the gaping wound. A drainage tube added insult to injury, a constant reminder of the trauma my foot had endured. Crutches became my new companions, transforming the one-simple act of walking into a great effort.

Back to reality in the hermit kingdom. Trying to turn over or move in bed was difficult and painful. There was always enough water for me to drink. You could tell by the taste if it had been boiled or not. After the water sat unconsumed for a period of time it developed a slimy, yucky looking gunk in the bottom of the teapot. From then on, I began the habit of not drinking the last little bit in a cup or glass, and that's a caution that still holds true today.

There was one time the water was cold and tasted good, compared to the water in the past. It did not take long for me to realize it had not been boiled. I acquired dysentery; I have never had the runs like that before or since. The bedpan happened to be on the floor beside the bed. I wasted no time getting out of bed, sitting down to squat, painful as that was. I could either deal with the pain getting to the pan in time, or deal with their anger at me because they had to clean up the vile mess I'd make in the bed.

I still had two open shrapnel wounds on my backside. One passed through me taking out half of my tailbone, a part of my pubic bone and my testicles. The other went in the bottom of my butt cheek, exiting out the top, leaving about an inch hole at the top, thankfully not damaging anything but muscle tissue.

The smile on my face in the photo on page 83 was calculated. If any photos were published anywhere in the world, they would eventually be sent to my parents. I wanted them to know I was okay. The doctor would come in every day to tend to my wounds. Most of the nurses with him would give me dirty looks, but every now and then they would smile, more than likely making fun of me.

Every one of the nurses appeared to have their chests wrapped in a tight piece of cloth like they were trying to keep their breasts from being noticed. None of them were very attractive, especially wearing no makeup, long white aprons, white hat, sporting a military uniform underneath.

For days after my surgery, the doctor would take forceps with a long strip of gauze, saturated with some yellow liquid substance like an oily salve ointment, and shove it down into my wounds. He forced the gauze as deep as possible, allowing the wound to heal from the inside out. I imagined this procedure was used for this type of wound even in the US. My wounds would take a very long time to heal, mostly because of the poor diet and second world medical procedures.

One day, about halfway through my healing process, the doctor pulled the gauze out of one of my wounds with a dark spot of something stuck to it. With the gauze hanging from the forceps tip, he turned it every direction, trying to determine what it could be. He did not try to show me, but I did see what he was looking at. I figured it was either a small blood clot or some type of insect crawling in the hole to get warm.

It didn't seem to matter either way, as far as he was concerned. He took a fresh piece of saturated gauze with his wonder drug and proceeded to stuff it down the hole.

I had a minor reaction to penicillin when I was in grade school and developed one hive so our family doctor suggested as a precaution, I should never take the drug again. That one hive drove me crazy for a few days and ever since then I have been labelled allergic to penicillin.

Unaware of that allergic condition, the doctor and nurses came in one day with a white milky vial of what I assumed to be penicillin. I began to panic, knowing an allergic reaction to anything in a foreign country is not good, especially in North Korea. No one there spoke English, so the translation procedure was by hand gestures and facial expression. It took some time but I eventually convinced the doctor not to give me the injection.

Another thing I was concerned about was the container the doctor carried his instruments in. It looked like a pan you would see in any hospital with one exception. They were not stainless steel which is not a big deal but the rust in the bottom of the pan was. Thankfully I never came down with anything out of the ordinary while in the hospital. I guess the extra iron did not matter.

I found out after I returned to the crew that my food at the hospital was slightly better than what they were being fed. I would receive an apple on a regular basis, worms and all. Rice, goat's milk, turnips, bread and butter, cabbage soup and of course the pig-fat soup were all part of my regular diet. The food was always the same, no variation from meal to meal.

We all take for granted how well we have it at home. In the US, we have three meals a day and there's always food in the pantry. I remember mom would fix fried chicken and mashed potatoes every Wednesday like clockwork. Like all youngsters, we had foods we did not like and complained about relentlessly, but we ate them anyway. We never went to bed hungry and always had food on the table.

CHAPTER 8
Lies, Lies, and More Lies

A few weeks after I was admitted to the hospital, Fetch came in with a higher-ranking officer carrying a paper for me to sign. It was the confession letter stating the USS Pueblo had entered their territorial waters under an act of espionage. At the bottom of the confession was Captain Bucher's signature and continuing on the next page were the signatures of all the crew.

I was unaware the crew had been tortured and forced to sign this false document. They insisted on me signing, and since I recognized

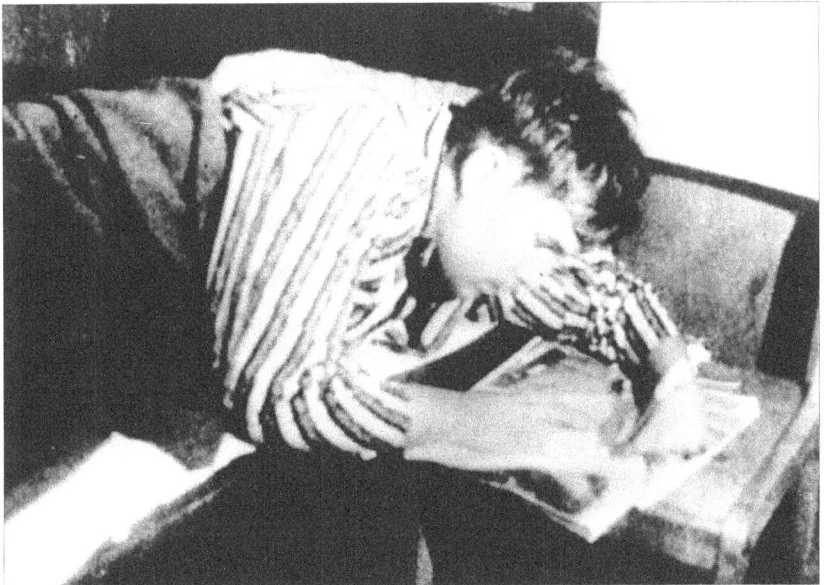

Woelk signing confession document in the North Korean hospital. North Korean propaganda photo.

several of my friends' signatures along with the skipper's, I signed it lying in my hospital bed.

Prior to that, and unbeknownst to me, Captain Bucher agreed to sign only after numerous brutal beatings. The North Koreans told him if he did not sign this confession, they were going to start executing the crew, beginning with the youngest. He had no alternative but to protect the crew and sign the fabricated statement. I learned after our release that Captain Bucher and several crewmen were nearly beaten to death before he broke down and agreed to sign their false confession.

Normally when being interrogated in a similar situation, the US military Code of Conduct allows you to give the enemy your name, rank, service number and date of birth. No disloyal statements and no harmful information could be shared. You were advised to resist coercion. But our service records were onboard Pueblo and had not been destroyed, so all this personnel information was compromised and could be used to determine if we were telling the truth or not. All crew were subjected to torture techniques like those used on prisoner of war victims in previous wars.

It was a big propaganda ordeal when they wanted something to telecast for their own people and the world to see. On the day of signing my "confession," they came in to set up all their cameras, brought in plants for the background, gave me new PJs, apples without worms, a clean set of sheets on the bed, an end table and all sorts of brand new, propaganda crap. I only knew they were up to something, but didn't know what it was. I never told them I played the guitar, but somehow, they knew because someone was standing in the doorway to my room holding up an old guitar, not my Gretsch, which was probably stolen.

I had my name in the guitar case left on the ship, and I'm sure this information would not be in my military records. After all the "look how well we are treating you BS" in front of the cameras was over, they let me have the guitar for an hour. I would have preferred a hamburger and fries. Could all this preferential treatment be a sign that I would be joining the crew about to be released? No, it was the start of a long period of inhuman violence.

Following the forcible full crew signing of this bogus document, the beatings and bullying threats to execute the crew stopped for a time.

The propaganda signing party was over for me. Plants were removed, propaganda reading material taken away, cameras left, PJs and apples remained but the guitar was taken away. It was back to the normal routine of daily injections, being poked with forceps, shoving long pieces of gauze into my wounds, hours of boredom and ugly nurses. No doubt praying daily and my faith in Jesus Christ had a lot to do with my ability to cope with homesickness and depression while in the hospital.

Thoughts would often cross my mind about what everyone back in the States was doing while we were in captivity. We knew our family and friends were worried about us, but as far as the rest of the world goes, everyone went along with their daily lives as if we did not exist, because we were a propaganda story half a world away and the Vietnam War was front page news everywhere.

As the year progressed, we assumed Pueblo had fallen off the front-page news. In 1968, there was a lot of turmoil in the United States with the assassinations of Robert F. Kennedy Sr. and Dr. Martin Luther King Jr., and the anti-Vietnam War riots. We had no definitive knowledge about any of that until we arrived home again, which was probably a good thing as we had enough to worry about. It took all we had inside to deal with everyday life, just trying to survive.

The deck of cards showing wear from constantly playing solitaire was never replaced. When my pack of cigarettes ran low, I would

receive another pack. When we were
released in December 1968, I managed
to smuggle out a pack of Kalmaigi cigarettes hidden in my coat.

The tobacco looked more like
chunks of wood than tobacco. Smoking the grapevine in the woods when
I was young was a much better experience than smoking Kalmaigis in North
Korea. I am sure the cigarettes were
more plant stalk than tobacco leaf. The

North Korean cigarettes. Steven Woelk photo.

crew was provided with one pack a day. Those who did not smoke
would divide their pack with the rest of the room. The cigarettes
were a North Korean brand, translated into English it means BULL
DUNG.

I kept track of my time in the hospital by marking the days on the
wall with a burnt match. Nothing was ever said to me for the marks
on the wall, which really surprised me. The walls were so filthy that I
suppose no one ever noticed the black marks.

The hard mattress and rice-stuffed pillow I slept on made it difficult to get a good night's sleep. My bed had been moved at some
point from being next to a wall to beside the cast iron steam register
below the only exterior window.

One night I propped my right leg up on the register for some heat.
It felt so good, I do not remember the rest of the night. The warmth
in my crotch had a soothing effect, I guess. When I think back over
the years this was the last time I remember sleeping through an entire night without tossing and turning or dreaming about that year
of my life. It was so comfortable I just forgot where I was for the
moment.

It may have been fate that I was moved over by the window during the month's full-moon phase. I would gaze out the upper window at the moon and extremely bright stars thinking about home. I wondered if Mom and Dad thought of me when they looked up at the same full moon hours later. Maybe this holy bond with my mother kept us thinking of each other over that year, but after our release Mom told me she would often look at the moon, think of me and pray for my well-being.

I was healing, but it was a slow process. Up until then, all I received were the injections in my arm on a daily basis. The nurses walked in one morning with a bottle of clear fluid, a large transfusion line (rubber hose), a large needle and a stand to hold the transfusion bottle.

They stuck the needle attached to the orange looking hose into my thigh for a transfusion. When the bottle was empty my leg had swollen twice its normal size. This was a new experience, never having had any type of transfusion, and I was petrified. No one seemed to be surprised by the appearance of my newly enlarged fat leg. It was nearing bedtime, I was exhausted, so I dozed off for the night wondering if I would be around the next morning. When I awoke my leg was back to its original size, which was a relief. I have no idea what they injected in me, but from that point on I started feeling better. After a day or so, I was even able to get out of bed and stand without assistance.

Near the end of my hospital stay, I knew I was getting well enough to be returned to where the crew was being held. I had noticed when the doctor stopped forcing gauze in me, that one of my wounds healed, leaving a water pocket under the skin. I was reluctant to tell the doctor about this new issue but knew if I were to return to the crew, it needed to be addressed.

Reluctantly, I asked my doctor to look at my wound again. He took one look, grabbed a pair of scissors out of his rusty ol' pan, and with one quick snip, bloody water gushed out—problem solved. At that point, it was back to stuffing the hole with gauze again. It had no impact on my return to the crew. It sure hurt like hell when he opened it up with the scissors without using any anesthetic.

I struggled walking when it was getting toward the end of my hospital stay. I was never allowed to leave the confinements of my private room, and for all I knew the door was locked anyway. Out of curiosity, I walked over to the door and looked up at the transom window. It was tilted at such an angle I could see my reflection. I was amazed at how much weight I had lost. Plus, I was having a really bad hair day. I was only allowed to take a washcloth or a sponge bath during my month and a half stay at the hospital. No, the nurses did not give me sponge baths.

RETURNING TO THE CREW

Suffering through forty-four days of confinement in a filthy hospital room, in constant pain, I crossed the milestone of my twentieth birthday not knowing what my future would entail. I spent that birthday alone, isolated in restriction with no cake, candles, or fanfare, just the heavy-set, flat-chested, ugly nurses. What a sad day to remember for sure.

They came in to prepare me to be moved yet again. There was a glimmer of hope as I returned to the crew, thinking our release from this godforsaken place meant freedom and a homeward journey. That thought evaporated, once again, as the guards bound me, blindfolded me, put me in a jeep, covered me with a blanket, and drove me to where the crew was sequestered.

Upon arrival, they helped me out of the jeep and allowed me to slowly walk to the door with Fetch, who was all smiles. Much to my surprise, the Pueblo officers were standing at the top of the stairs to greet me. The climb up those stairs was slow and painful. I grabbed onto the rail, pulling myself along, but managed to make it without any assistance. The last time they had seen me, I was bedridden with my injuries, so this was a welcome sight.

The guards would not allow anyone to assist me on this climb. I could see Captain Bucher and the officers were glad to see me but still concerned about my condition. I had no idea they were kept in the dark about the extent of my injuries or that I was in the hospital. I told them that I was doing okay, still in a healing process, but I had lost the ol' family jewels. They were in total shock! Time for me to get into the daily routine with the rest of the crew.

They put me in a room with seven other crewmen, Mac, Bob Chicca, Charlie Crandell, Dale Rigby, Rodney, Angelo, and another Bob to round it out to eight. Everyone had the same color and style of clothes to wear every day. I received my new set of clothes so I blended in with the rest of the guys. We each had our own bed, a chair and a little nightstand to store what few possessions we had.

When I opened the bottom door to my nightstand for the first time, there were my Navy dungarees and boots I was wearing when the ship was attacked. My blood-soaked shirt and dungarees had several jagged holes torn by the shrapnel. When I unfolded my pants, something grey in color and looking like a rock fell out on the floor. It was a little less than an inch wide, about two inches long and less than a quarter-inch thick but no weight to it. It was a piece of bone. I had no idea what part of me it came from. I held onto it as a souvenir for the longest time, until one day when we anticipated a shakedown of our room. It was best not to have anything in our possession, other than what the North Koreans gave us, so I pitched it the next time we went outside.

The daily barracks life for me with the crew was about to start. I had not been part of the beatings or torture most of the crew had faced up to that time. The beatings had stopped briefly after confessions were signed by everyone. Every day was pretty much the same thing, days of boredom with hours of terror.

We would all get up at a certain time, grab a cigarette off the table, get dressed, go to the bathroom, then walk down the hall to breakfast. All the meals were served in a small room by a couple of our crewmen who dished out what was brought to them from the Korean cooks in the main kitchen.

An electric hot plate was provided for them to warm up whatever needed to be reheated. Our food consisted of rice in every meal, cabbage/turnip/pig-fat soup, and tolerable air-dried fish when it was fresh; but not very edible when it started turning rancid. We called it sewer trout.

During harvest season, fresh vegetables were turned into kimchi. Fresh kimchi tastes good before they bury it in the ground in large vats. Fresh, it was nutritional, but when taken out of the ground after it had aged, it was an acquired taste. I did not like it. Kimchi season was the only time we received fresh veggies. We did not see where the urns of kimchi were buried, but I assume it was on the property nearby.

Bread was sometimes served with butter, probably churned on site with black streaks through it, possibly from the turning crank grease. The butter was okay fresh, but it would also turn rancid over time. There was no refrigeration to preserve food. We had a grayish-looking rice cake that was extremely malleable with a fairly good taste to it.

Sardines were served occasionally, but the Korean brand was not so good. Russian sardines were served a couple times, and they were very good. When the soup was being dished out, we would find flies, worms, nails and rocks, just to name a few of our tasty surprises. We were never quite desperate enough to eat nature's natural protein, the maggots.

Soon after returning to the crew, I was informed by one of my roommates that they did not trust me at first. They were concerned I might have been brainwashed, then planted with the crew to get information. I understood their uncertainty, but imagine not being trusted because I had been isolated from them for so long. I do not remember anyone keeping their distance from me, but it's still unnerving. I guess they realized I was still a Midwest, small-town kid from Kansas, and they eventually accepted me.

PROPAGANDA LETTERS HOME

After the North Koreans had finished with the forced confessions, they focused us on writing propaganda letters to government officials and our families. All letters were highly censored to the extent they told us what to write: just the truth, the whole truth and nothing but the truth according to the North Korean propaganda ministry. The North Koreans manipulated Pueblo's navigational charts to show the world we had entered their territorial waters. We learned, as we got to know our captors, their English-language education instructors apparently left out double meanings of words, slang and sarcasm. We took advantage of this by adding words to our letters that either did not mean anything or had a meaning they did not comprehend.

We would use names of deceased family members, people who did not exist, television cartoon and movie characters, anything the North Koreans could not verify. We all wanted to let our loved ones know we were alive and doing well, but we also wanted to get the message across not to believe anything being sent.

My parents had not been notified that I was wounded until the middle of the year. When I wrote to Mom and Dad, I tried to explain the extent of my injuries. I did not fully understand why, but the North Koreans would not allow me to mention my injuries.

My parents were told one of the crew had been killed and one of us lost a leg. Exactly when the word finally got out I don't know, but for a long time, no one knew Duane Hodges was the crewman killed or who the crewmen were that sustained wounds during the attack.

It wasn't until much later in the year, that propaganda photos and videos of the crew were sent through North Korean allies to world news organizations. Their efforts to solicit support for their so-called leniency toward the crew, in response to the dastardly deed we imposed on the North Korean people, was carefully orchestrated.

The photo taken of me sitting in my hospital bed next to the doctor was sent to my parents verifying for them that I was alive, but it did not convince them I had not lost my right leg. It appeared my right leg was missing up to my hip. I always had a natural smile but if these photos were being sent to the world to see, I made a point to smile, hoping it would indicate to my parents that I was alive and doing okay.

During our welcome-home Christmas party months later, I told Dad the extent of my injuries. When we had finished eating, like everyone else in the room, we were all catching up on what we had missed the past year. Dad and I went for a walk, leaving Mom alone at the table for a few minutes.

We walked down a hallway toward the bathrooms, a quiet area for the time being. I began to tell him what had happened from the time I was wounded until I was released from the hospital. I could see him getting very emotional, but I needed to tell him. I did not feel comfortable telling Mom at the time, and I thought it would be best if Dad told her. We gathered our composure and headed back to the table to join Mom. We never spoke about my time in Korea again.

CHAPTER 9
The Farm

We called it "The Farm." It appeared to be some type of athletic housing facility for special events. The three-story stone building with marble walls in the hallways and alcoves was probably impressive to visitors who stayed there but not to us. The floorboards were the same as in my hospital room, dirty in appearance with quarter-inch spaces between each board.

The area we were allowed to access outside was fairly large. It was the size of a soccer field surrounded by an oval track. This may have been where the visiting teams competed while staying in this same building. The size of the other rooms or how many were on each floor was not disclosed at the time, as far as I can remember.

Our room on the third floor was approximately 15' x 15', with a set of windows that could be opened. There was a commons area down the hall with a stairway in the middle going down to the next floor, with wings on either side of the stairs where our rooms were located. Our room was to the right as you topped the stairs. The eight of us were in the last room on the left side at the end of the hallway.

The crew occupied at least two of the floors, with the officers on the second floor. The toilets and bathing area were located on another floor as well. The commons area in front of the stairway was used for the guards to mingle, monitor our limited movements and play ping-pong.

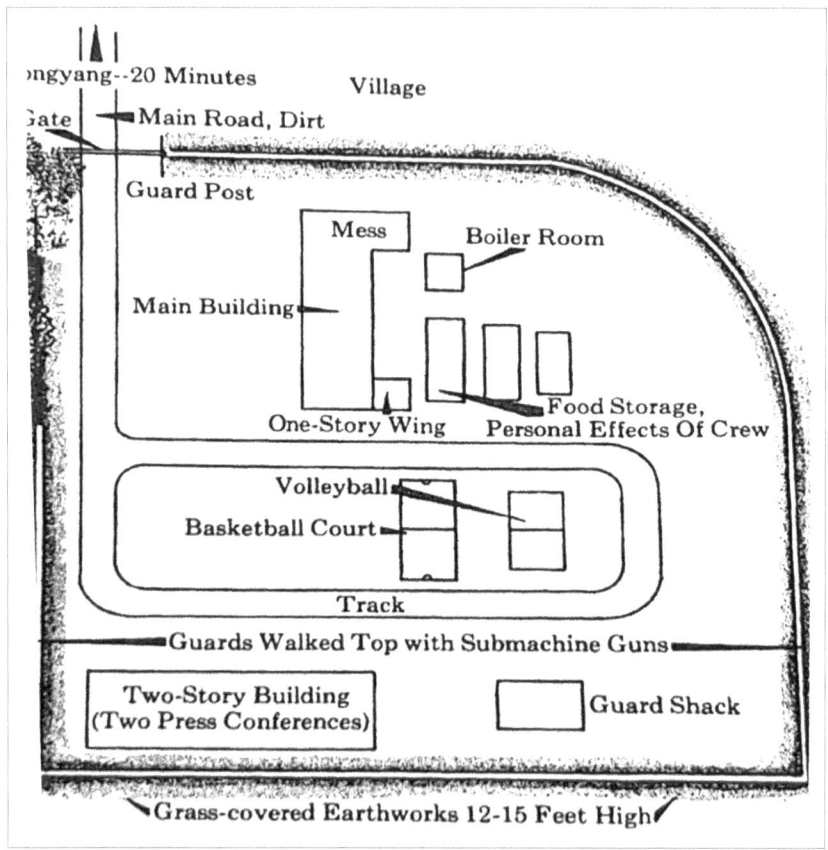

Illustration by George Linyear, taken from Last Voyage of the Pueblo.

A North Korean officer sat at a desk located in this open area 24/7. Later in captivity, we were allowed to play ping-pong, one room at a time, when weather would not permit us to go outside. For recreation in our rooms, we had playing cards, and a chess game. Bob Chicca taught me how to play chess, but I never did get very good at the game.

The soccer field had a volleyball net set up and a ball was provided to use. Those who did not want to play soccer played tag football. Those who did not want to play either sport would walk and talk. This was a good time to catch up on rumors and scheme ways to be a real pain in their ass. Sometimes we got away with our shenanigans. There were those times we would get thumped, but it was worth it.

The football games were discontinued due to the number of crewmen who were getting minor injuries. Our captors did not want us to hurt ourselves. They reserved the right to beat us up. We were allowed outside for no more than thirty minutes at a time, weather permitting.

Our room, like all the other rooms, exhibited a broad variety of religious beliefs. Protestant, Mormon and Catholic were prevalent in our room. You would think there would be religious arguments but there were not. There were plenty of arguments about everything else

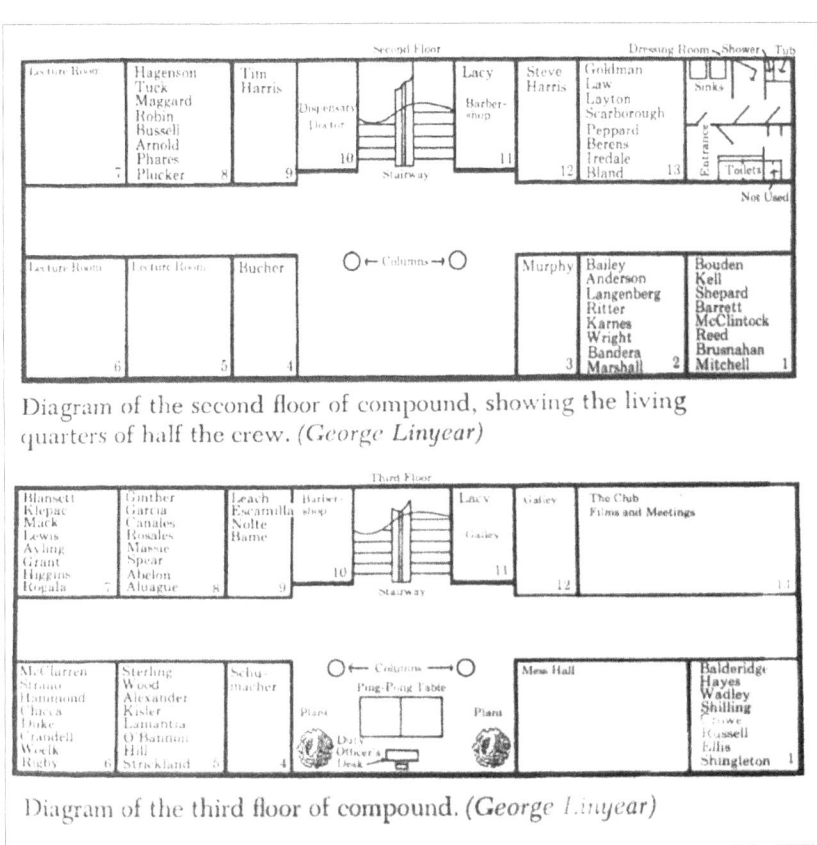

Diagram of the second floor of compound, showing the living quarters of half the crew. (George Linyear)

Diagram of the third floor of compound. (George Linyear)

Illustration by George Linyear, taken from Last Voyage of the Pueblo.

imaginable, but not religion. We did not hold group prayer sessions, I would imagine due to the broad religious beliefs.

Individual prayer may not have been apparent but was definitely going on. We all respected each other's religious backgrounds and beliefs. As for me, I prayed daily for my well-being. I never prayed for a miracle, but rather for me to have the ability to cope with anything that may alter the course of my life, one day at a time.

I quit smoking while in captivity for a couple of reasons. Every morning when we got up, everyone would make a mad rush to the cigarettes on the table. It was almost getting to the point they would fight over who could get one in their mouth and lit first. I did not need that in my life. As I explained earlier, their cigarettes were not like anything we had ever smoked before; they tasted terrible.

I never smoked again, but later in life I did take up another tobacco habit much harder to quit than smoking, chewing Skoal. I managed to quit but would start again tomorrow if it wasn't so bad for your health. I stopped when my dentist told me, "You'll quit when your lower teeth fall out." OKAY!

PRIVILEGES

In a different kind of roller coaster experience than riding rough seas, the mood of the North Koreans was up and down. One day they would terrorize us and the next they would leave us alone. Every time they wanted something, if we refused, our privileges were taken away and we would not be allowed to go outside. If we resisted long enough, beatings and threats would start again. When they got what they wanted, we earned privileges back and the same held true for the quality of food they provided.

If there was to be a propaganda shoot or press conference, the food was better and displayed for all the world to see how well we were being treated. This included cookies, rice wine, bowls of fruit

From r to l: Captain Bucher, XO Edward Murphy, Steve Harris, Gene Lacy, Ralph McClintock, Charles Law, and Bob Hammond facing the press. North Korean propaganda photo.

without the worms, and even cigarettes of better quality, probably from Russia. All this was for show in front of the cameras and international reporters. Once the camera lights were turned off and the press departed, the nice-looking food also disappeared.

They would show extremely anti-American movies once a week. Most reenacted war battles they claimed were war atrocities by South Koreans and Americans. North Korea won every battle and their fearless leader, Kim Il Sung, was their glorious hero who they believed fought in every one of them.

On two separate occasions, we were taken on field trips. The first was to a war museum that depicted war atrocities, which according to them, were against the North Koreans by the US. They thought we would be convinced they were being slaughtered by our Army, but we did not interpret their propaganda this way. War is hell no matter what side you are on.

The other trip was to a very large arena filled with Koreans. There were hundreds of participants on the field and in the stands. The people in the audience would put on a show using large colorful flash-cards. The dancers on the floor of the arena wore elaborate, colorful costumes. It was quite impressive, but it still had an anti-US theme in the entire production. The North Koreans thought by treating us to a night out on the town, we would believe they were a caring society. This so-called act of kindness could also imply that talks between the US and North Korea were going well. The next day it was back to the routine of kicking the crap out of us.

This kept us on edge all the time, the ups and downs of not know-ing what to expect from day to day. You may not be targeted physi-cally, but mentally, that has a lasting effect.

Anytime we left the room, we were subjected to mock executions with our captors using a handgun or dry firing their AK-47s at our heads. They also kicked us, hit us with their fists, and karate chopped us using their hard-as-steel, calloused hands. One of their favorite pastimes was to make us stand at attention in the hallway lined up to go to the bathroom. That was when they unleashed the most severe torment. The guards were out of sight of the officers in charge, so they would have a hay day harassing us. There was nothing we could do but stand at attention or get a physical beating.

We took baths and washed our own clothes once a week. Our baths were taken down on the second floor where the bathroom was located. They instructed us to strip down, take a bucket of hot water out of a large concrete basin, and dump it over our entire body. Soap up, scrub down, then rinse off with a second bucket. We were limited to two pails of hot water each; we assumed they bathed in the same manner eight at a time. When sixteen buckets of water were drawn out of the basin, it was empty.

The first time I was able to get my entire body wet was when the bandages finally came off. Getting wet all over my body with hot water felt so good. A month and a half of cleaning up with a pan of water and a rag left a lot to be desired, especially in a bedridden state dealing with bandages and open wounds.

A North Korean General in charge of us reported back to Kim Il Sung, their god of the DPRK. He would gather us all in a large room to lecture us for hours at a time using an interpreter. He would try to convince us how good they were and how bad we were. He would tell us, "Your government is bad for not admitting you penetrated North Korean territorial waters while conducting espionage." He was a very scary person, and even the North Korean guards and officers feared him.

During the early period of our incarceration, General C, or Super C, the name he was sometimes tagged with, or one of the interpreters, commented, "We are not afraid of the USS Enterprise." We assumed from this remark that the Enterprise must be sitting somewhere off the coast or steaming in our direction.

We assumed all of the guards and officers understood at least some of the English language, so we were careful about what we said around them. Most of the officers, or anyone who was educated in another country, more than likely knew the English language fluently. The only North Korean we knew who spoke English very well was Fetch. We had names for all of the guards and officers. Some names varied from room to room. We would not always know who they would be referring to when they came up in conversation.

The crew eventually received basic medical treatment when someone came down with a virus or wound that could be potentially serious. Some crewmen developed terrible sores on their skin due to poor nutrition and unsanitary conditions. The medical equipment they used on us was in the same building. The chest X-ray made no sense, but they did it anyway, probably because of the nasty cigarettes.

The X-ray machine was a huge black beast. When they turned it on to take the image, it sounded like it just kept zapping you with radiation. One crewman was having trouble with his eyesight. They treated him by sticking needles into his eyeballs. He became blind shortly after our release.

Midsummer 1968, I came down with an unshakable episode of tonsillitis. It meant seeing my ol' doctor friend again. He determined my tonsils would have to be removed. Unbeknownst to me about what was soon to take place, the guards escorted me out of my room to where they had the X-ray machine. I was put into a chair, motioned to open my mouth. He then took what looked like kite string out of his little bag of tricks. It was the same type of string they used to suture our wounds previously. Uh-oh!

He sutured a string to each tonsil, then put this clamping device down my throat. With a crunching sound the left tonsil came out when they pulled on the string. They performed the same procedure to the other tonsil. Once again, no anesthetic was used for this procedure.

Back home, after a tonsillectomy procedure, you could have ice cream to soothe the throat. Not in the DPRK; their choice was pig fat soup.

ESCAPE PLAN

I am sure the thought of trying to escape was on everyone's mind at some point during captivity. Our room decided to take that thought seriously. When looking out of our third-story room window, we could see a monument off in the distance. Propaganda magazines contained photos of their prized monuments and we determined this winged horse monument was the one photographed in an article.

Once we had our bearings, confirming where we were in Pyong-yang, a plan was hatched. I am not sure how it was determined what direction we were from the monument or where we were in the city, but my roomies were a lot smarter than I when it came to this dead-reckoning guestimate.

It would take some time for a food supply to be gathered. The only nonperishable item we were being fed was dried squid. Now imagine trying to take a bite out of a dry chamois. It was dry, tough to chew and tasted like crap. So I would say, "Yes, you can have my share, does not bother me in the slightest."

To hide this stash, we needed an inconspicuous location in our room. Prying up a loose board in the floor, we found a space where small items could be hidden. The fish could have been used, since it was not refrigerated anyway, but it could not be stored under the floor without being detected by its foul odor.

Room searches were becoming more frequent, so it was decided to destroy the food stash and abandon the plan of escape. An American trying to make his way inconspicuously through Pyong-yang would be nearly impossible. We rationalized that this small band of escapees wearing prison outfits probably wouldn't get very far and the consequences would be worse than the treatment we had received up to that point.

KEEPING OUR MINDS OCCUPIED

There was a time during our captivity when several of the CTs thought about trying to make a radio. We knew we would not be able to transmit, but maybe it could be used to receive news. The two Korean linguists in our room were not familiar with the North Koreans' dialect but could understand enough to help in the interpretation of key words.

When there are a bunch of guys who know how electronics work, I guess anything is possible. We all started looking for items needed for the task whenever we were outside. The outdoor space where we were allowed to engage in sports gave us a large area to search. We were not permitted freedom to roam the entire area but could cover a lot of ground before the guards became suspicious. I believe we found a piece of wood for a core, some wire and a piece of metal for the crystal. A radio, then a TV, the possibilities were unlimited! Well maybe not, but it sure kept our minds occupied. We gave up hope of finding anything useful after poking around for a while.

The North Koreans graciously provided each of us with a little two-inch blade pocketknife that was supposed to be used for cleaning our fingernails, I guess. We found a stone outside that could be used to sharpen this little beast.

Bob Chicca found a piece of wood he confiscated from the playground and started whittling a miniature ship. He did a remarkable job of carving this five-inch piece of wood into a piece of art. He hid it under the loose board in the floor so the guards would not find it. We had a feeling another shakedown was coming so Bob thought it best to destroy his creation before it was found. It was just one of the ways to keep the mind busy and pass time.

My mind began drifting off to thinking about how music influenced my life several years before entering the military. Back in time when I started playing music, I met so many people along the way. No one else in my room had the same musical interests as me. I would sit in silence reminiscing about the past, much like I did when I was alone in the hospital. The four of us who played in the band together never had any music lessons to speak of, we just started playing by ourselves with family members, or getting help along the way from other musicians.

I would put Johnny Cash records on the stereo to play along with his lead guitar player Luther Perkins. Chet Atkins was another influence in my budding guitar-playing days. But I could not quite get the ol' fingers to follow along using his style. I could play a couple of his songs, but they were not even close to the master's rendition.

My singing ability came naturally. I listened to other country artists, trying to mimic their singing style, never trying to sound like them, but would hear the different ways they controlled their voices. Thinking about the good times I played with the band was a useful way to take my mind off boredom and terror that was happening all around me.

Some of my crew members started writing down words on toilet paper to all the songs they could remember. If someone could not remember words to a particular song, you could always bet that at least one of this crew of 82 could come up with something close.

Our third-floor room had a window covered with paper, but the edges could be pulled back to see the surrounding countryside in front of the facility. Even though we were in or close to Pyongyang, there were large rice fields as far as we could see off to the horizon, before disappearing over the hill.

In the early spring, workers would be out planting new stalks of rice in the neatly prepared soil. Loudspeakers were placed all around the field on poles blaring a voice all day long when the workers were present. We were unable to understand what they were saying, but we assumed it was propaganda telling the workers how great Kim Il Sung was as their leader. A small tractor sat off to the side of the fields, but most of the field work was done by hand. The fields were flooded with water for the growing season, then drained dry for the fall harvest.

When it was time to harvest, scythes were used to cut the stalks. They bundled and stood them on end to be picked up later. The small tractor hitched with a trailer was driven out on the field to pick up the bundles. We could not see where the stalks were taken.

It was a sight to see a complete rice harvest season from planting to harvest. Rice, wheat, corn, and many other grains were probably planted and harvested the same way back in the States by our ancestors. North Korea was so far behind the times, but its people were taught they had the most sophisticated equipment and methods in the world.

The fish we were served was dried outside on what looked like clotheslines located on the ground level below our window. Fish hung there for a few weeks before being removed for consumption. The fish, rather oily, tasted okay when served freshly dried, but when it was nearing its expiration date, it had a foul odor and foul taste as well.

Another great American pastime for our room was to see how many of the hundreds of houseflies buzzing around we could kill in a day. We would kill the flies, collect them, then show the guards our accomplishment each day. Some of the guards thought it amusing. Some of them thought we were crazy. A thread from our clothes was tied to a fly's body then let loose to fly around the room.

If you use your imagination, you can come up with all sorts of ways to pass time.

Occasionally we received an apple with our meals, wormy, but healthy. A couple of the guys in my room thought they would try their hand in starting an apple orchard, but we thought it best to start with just one tree. I don't recall what we planted the seed in at first but to everybody's surprise the seed sprouted, growing into this neat little six-inch apple tree. The guards were pleased we were trying to raise our own fruit.

At a time in our lives that we were not sure what was going on, we decided to do something with the apple tree. We did not want them to have the satisfaction of having this precious little tree we had started from seed. We all took turns peeing on it in hopes it would last just long enough until we were gone. Then they would think we had a green thumb but when they took over it died.

Every day was a new day with a new topic to talk about. You never knew whether it was going to be a day of harassment, a good day when most of us would be in good spirits, or another day of terror. We were generally in good spirits, but no one could be upbeat all the time. When someone was down or showing signs of depression, there would always be a few of us having a good day to pick him up.

CHAPTER 10
Hawaiian Good Luck Sign

Back row, l to r: Mac, Bob, Rodney, Dale. Front row l to r: Charlie, Bob, Angelo and Steven. Notice the middle finger. North Korean propaganda photo.

At one point during the showing of a Korean dis-information film, a shipmate noticed a newsreel showing Korean athletes participating in an international event where several individuals in the crowd gave the North Korean cameraman the middle finger. We had no idea what they were saying or what they were angry about. We figured if they could get away with it maybe this would be another way for us to get our message out.

Letting everyone at home know we were being forced to parade before these cameras and recite scripted comments, was important to us. Group photos taken in every room had at least one crew member displaying the middle finger. When propaganda photos and movies were taken by news reporters, someone would inconspicuously extend their middle finger. The North Koreans started to inquire about its meaning, so we told them it was a Hawaiian good luck sign.

They bought it.

We were hoping our families and government would pick up on the signal. What we did not expect was that the meaning of the middle finger would be published in *Time* magazine by an overzealous reporter. The resultant repercussions we suffered as a direct result were almost unbearable.

Time running a story about our plight, showing the pictures and explaining our symbol of defiance was certainly what led to "Hell Week." The most rewarding and damaging tool in our arsenal as incarcerated men was snuffed out guilelessly by *Time*. It was only a matter of time before the North Koreans learned that we were insulting them with the Hawaiian Good Luck sign, and they got pissed.

HELL WEEK

The North Koreans focused their wrath mainly on the crewmen who used the finger gesture in the photos and film clips. But we all suffered. Everyone took a beating. From eight to a room, they added two and crowded each room with ten of us. The beds and chairs in each room were rearranged with five beds on each side of the room and a straight chair at the end of each bed. This left just enough room for the guards to walk down the center while we were sitting in the chairs.

Guards would walk between us and take advantage of us in whatever way they chose at the time. We were forced to put our chins on our chests looking down the entire day and into the night. If they were about to clobber us, we could not see it coming with our heads down. The lights were left on throughout the day and night. The heat was turned off twenty-four hours a day. The only time we were allowed to leave the room was either to go to the bathroom as a group, to eat, or be beaten.

Before Hell Week, I was only kicked once by a guard while standing at attention and waiting in the hallway to go to the bathroom. During Hell Week, I received several blows to the side of my head, kicks to the stomach, and a karate chop on the neck. In the days to come, there was another round of blows from the guard we called "The Bear." I was hit in the head several times, kicked in the stomach again, once in the groin, and in my thigh and shin. The second time, he hit me in the neck, causing damage that has plagued me ever since, a constant reminder of his brutality. The Bear's palm was so calloused it felt like a 2 x 4 when he hit me.

This is a constant reminder of the brutality we all endured. It only takes one blow to cause pain for the rest of your life. When The Bear came into our room on another occasion, he knocked me out of the chair to the floor. We tried to show no emotion, giving them less satisfaction for their actions. I rolled over, got up, sat back in the chair and resumed the heads-down position. I did not want to give him the opportunity to start kicking me on the floor.

Doors were left open 24/7. We could not see or even dare look at what was taking place in the room across the hall from us. Sounds coming from beyond our door were unnerving. We would hear screaming and hollering, and chairs being thrown around. The sounds of someone getting knocked around lasted all day and into the night.

Whether the North Koreans were beating one of us or making sounds to make us think someone was being beaten, we could not tell. The bruises and black eyes told the majority of the story that the crew was getting beaten brutally. The psychological effect of this continuing noise was enough to crush our spirits. It had the desired effect they were looking for.

One crewman decided to take his own life during Hell Week. He broke a mirror that was handed out to each of us near the beginning of imprisonment, and tried to cut both wrists. It was my understanding he was trying to send a message to our attackers, "How far are you really willing to go, before you have another death to explain?" Thank goodness his attempt failed.

Crewmen who displayed the finger in the photos were beaten so badly you could hardly identify them by looking at their faces. We were not going to be able to take much more of that type of treatment. If it did not end soon, one or more of us was likely going to be killed.

Suddenly, Hell Week ended as quickly as it started and those who were beaten severely were quickly patched up to look almost normal.

NEGOTIATIONS FOR OUR RELEASE

The Korean officers would often hint if something was about to take place. We came close to heading home once before but apparently something fell through in the negotiations. When Hell Week ended abruptly, we suspected something else was up.

As alluded to in the first chapter piece from ADST, negotiations for our release were held at Panmunjom by the Army. Navy Admiral Smith was replaced by Army General Gilbert H. Woodward, Senior Member, United States Command Military Commission. General Woodward, an experienced negotiator with the North Koreans, was familiar with their tactics so he was assigned to deal with them instead of the less experienced Naval officer.

The Navy lacked the negotiating-table knowledge needed to deal with these unpredictable animals. Getting someone up to speed with the tactics and behavior of the North Koreans would slow down the process and most assuredly come up short of the goal. In the end, it still took General Woodward nearly eleven months to successfully get a release of all sailors.

The North Korean demands were to prepare a document stating the US Government would apologize for violating their territorial waters, admit we were conducting espionage, and assure that it would never happen again.

Admission of being inside their territorial waters is where the stalemate occurred between the United States and North Korea, developing into a bitter disagreement. There were times the North Koreans would get upset and either would not show up for scheduled meetings or walk away from the talks in progress.

The United States would not admit that Pueblo crossed over into North Korea's territorial waters. Under pressure and with the North Koreans driving the narrative, the US negotiating team needed to find another way to make our release happen.

Apparently, the wife of a member of the negotiating panel came up with a possible solution. She suggested the US should make a

US Navy at the Panmunjom negotiating table; middle right, US Army General Gilbert H. Woodward, senior member, United States Command Military Commission. US Navy photo.

statement prior to signing the confession that the United States was signing the confession to release the crew and to release the crew only. The document was written up and presented to the North Korean side of the table.

Nothing could be decided at Panmunjom by the North Koreans until the document was approved by Kim Il Sung, their leader. This back-and-forth process intentionally slowed down all negotiations. This statement was made, "This document is being signed to release the crew and to release the crew only."

Actual statement signed by General Woodward to secure the release of the PUEBLO crew:

To the Government of the Democratic People's Republic of Korea

The Government of the United States of America,

Acknowledging the validity of the confessions of the crew of the USS "Pueblo" and the documents of evidence produced by the representative of the Government of the Democratic People's Republic of Korea to the effect that the ship, which was seized by the self-defesce measures of the vessels of the Korean People's Army in the territorial waters of the Democratic People's Republic of Korea on January 23, 1968, had illegally intruded into the territorial waters of the Democratic People's Republic of Korea on many occasions and conducted espionage activities of spying out important military and state secrets of the Democratic People's Republic of Korea,

Shoulders full responsibility and solemnly apologizes for the grave acts of espionage of the U.S. ship against the Democratic People's Republic of Korea after having intruded into the territorial waters of the Democratic People's Republic of Korea,

And gives firm assurance that no U.S. ships will intrude again in future into the territorial waters of the Democratic People's Republic of Korea,

Meanwhile, the Government of the United States of America earnestly requests that the Government of the Democratic People's Republic of Korea deal leniently with the former crew members of the USS "Pueblo" confiscated by the Democratic People's Republic of Korea side, taking into consideration that these crew members have confessed honestly to their crimes and petitioned the Government of the Democratic People's Republic of Korea for leniency.

Simultaneously with the signing of this document, the undersigned acknowledges receipt of 82 crew members of the "Pueblo" and one corpse.

On behalf of the Government of
the United States of America

Gilbert H. Woodward
Major General
United States Army
23 December 1968

Signed US pacification letter to gain release of Pueblo crew.

The document was drawn up to release the crew, General Woodward signed, Kim Il Sung signed, and done deal.

That created a problem for the North Koreans. They held 82 men, whom they had been beating the hell out of for more than a week. How were they going to get the crew of the Pueblo cleaned up in time to be presentable enough to send home?

I, along with many of the crew, believed someone was watching over us who would communicate with the American side. The word

Pueblo crewmen walk spaced approximately ten feet apart while the remaining crew waits at the far end of the bridge. Stars and Stripes photo.

somehow got out that the crew was in urgent need of getting out of there. Someone was going to die if circumstances did not change and that change needed to happen soon.

ON OUR WAY TO FREEDOM

Some say we were taken away by train, then buses. I am sure they were right about the train, but all I remember was the bus ride. The windows on the bus were papered over making it difficult to see out—not impossible, just difficult. When they stopped driving, we were parked at the north end of what we thought was the Bridge of No Return. Our captors had still not told us we were being released, and we did not know for sure where they had taken us.

The 38th parallel at Panmunjom has been the cease-fire border between North and South Korea since 27 July, 1953, when the Armistice was initially signed. It did not officially end the war but merely established a cease-fire. To this day, there remains no formal peace treaty between the United States and North Korea, leaving the Korean Peninsula technically in a state of war.

Our release had been negotiated at Panmunjom in a room divided in half. North Korea and China were on one side, with the United States on the other side of the table. South Korea, as I mentioned earlier, was not invited nor permitted to participate in these negotiations.

Eleven months of physical torture by the North Koreans had finally come to an end. The mental part would continue for most if not all of my crew members. The psychological effects have been a life lasting burden.

After leaving the bus to cross the bridge, I was in a daze. I do not remember getting off the bus or walking across the bridge. Our minds could not process all that was happening. From being terrorized and beaten, to seeing freedom come closer with each step on that bridge.

We were instructed to walk in single file across the narrow concrete bridge, spaced a good distance from each other. Captain Bucher ordered us not to turn around, make any gestures or say anything while walking to freedom. Do not do anything to jeopardize your fellow crewmen behind you from getting out of this hell hole. The Bear, our most feared guard, went up to one of my fellow crewmen who continuously defied The Bear, in perfect English, called him out by name told him, "Do not ever return to North Korea."

The release went off without any problems as we walked slowly, single file, quietly and stunned, across the bridge. Forty-eight hours prior to this release, we were brutally and harshly beaten. Now, by a miracle, we all walked to our freedom. We were all a bit numb walking across the bridge after an eleven-month-long ordeal.

Captain Bucher had to identify Duane Hodges' remains prior to his wooden coffin being carried across the bridge, before the rest of us were released. Duane was then placed in an Army ambulance at the end of the bridge and taken away before we could start our walk to freedom. Army buses were backed up to the freedom side of the "Bridge of No Return."

CREW ROSTER CHECKLIST

Once across the bridge, after the longest walk of my life, on the South Korean side, I was greeted by a Navy Lt. Commander who welcomed me home. Then he asked for my name. Our names were compared to the ships roster, whereupon he checked off names one at a time.

A Navy photographer was snapping pictures of all of us as fast as he could load the camera to record this time in history. Keep in

Woelk giving his name at the checkpoint on South Korean soil. US Navy photo.

mind that this was back in the day when military photography used black-and-white film. It was a long time before digital photography.

The Navy taking photos was a lot different than the North Koreans taking photos of us in captivity. Would you believe, I say cynically, that not one of us decided to make North Korea his permanent home for the rest of his life? Once we were checked off the list, in a state of shock, unbelief, etc., the bus caravan took us to the 121st Air Evacuation Hospital at Panmunjom, a short distance from the bridge. There, we were fed ham and cheese sandwiches and chicken noodle soup. The Army 121st Evacuation Hospital issued us hospital clothes after we all showered. After sprucing up, we were all examined by a doctor to make sure we were well enough to make the trip home.

Submariner jumpsuits and Pueblo ball caps were issued prior to attending a church service that evening. On our first night of freedom in eleven months, we finally slept in decent beds with normal pillows. We could have cared less if they were hospital beds. The sheets were clean, the mattress and pillow were soft. No hard mattresses, rice pillows or fear of a guard busting through the door in a rage. We were one step closer to being out of harm's way and heading home.

Speaking of the cap, the USS Pueblo hat I wear is more than just a piece of clothing; it's a badge of honor, a symbol of a shared experience unlike any other. It invariably sparks conversations, but sometimes those conversations take an unexpected turn. I've lost count of the times someone has made their way to my side with a wide grin on their face, claiming they had a buddy or a cousin who served on the Pueblo. Names would be thrown out, stories fabricated, and I'd listen patiently, with a small smile playing on my lips.

We, the crew of the Pueblo, were a tight-knit group. After all, when you're held captive for eleven months, you get to know your shipmates intimately. We shared meals together, endured hardships together, and

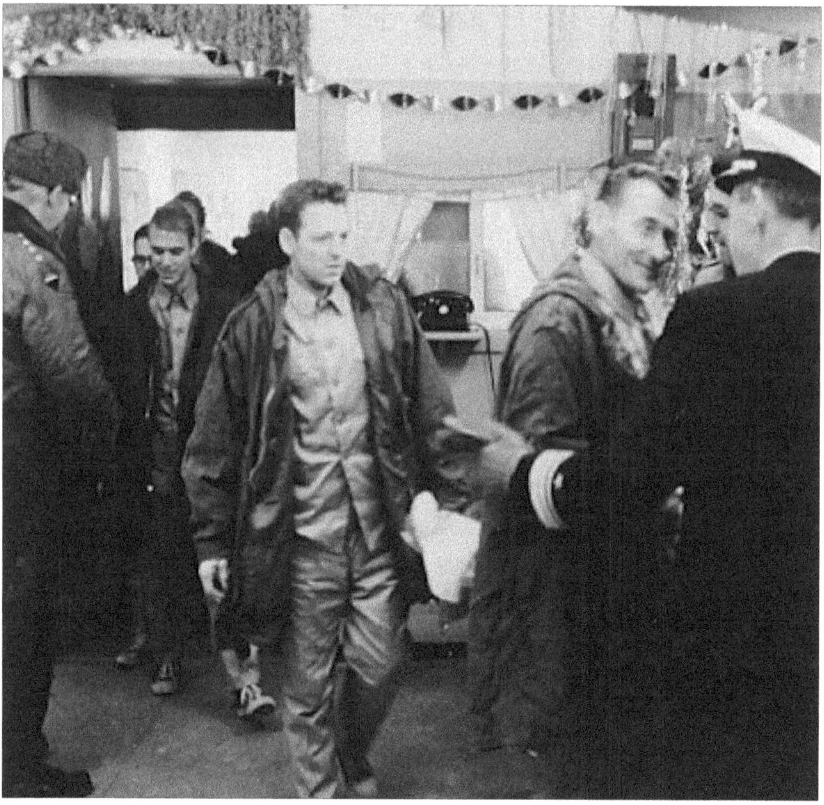

Repatriation and crew leaving a US Army bus following their release from captivity. US Navy photos.

emerged with an unbreakable bond. So, when someone throws out a name I don't recognize, it's a gentle reminder that there are imposters out there, people who crave a connection to something they have never experienced. There are better ways to make that connection than stealing someone's honor or pretending to be someone else.

Humor became a lifeline during our captivity, a way to maintain sanity amidst the uncertainty. It's a coping mechanism I continue to use today. So, when faced with these "wannabees," a little humor goes a long way. A wink, a smile, and a kind, "There must be some confusion there," usually ends the conversation on a light note. But for those genuine connections, veterans who served or legitimate family relationships, the ensuing conversations are filled with stories shared and a welcome camaraderie. Friendships are borne that way. Those are the moments I truly cherish.

MEMORIAL FOR DUANE HODGES

Prior to leaving Panmunjom, I was invited to attend a tarmac memorial service for Duane. This would be a last opportunity, on Korean soil, to pay my final respects to my best friend. Unfortunately, I was unable to attend his funeral in Creswell, Oregon, after we arrived home, due to the debriefing process we were drawn through with the Navy. I am far left under the American flag in the photo on the next page.

After the short memorial, Duane's body was loaded onto one of the planes that would take us all home together.

HOMEWARD BOUND

The crew at Panmunjom was assembled, loaded onto Hueys and flown to where the planes were parked, near Duane's memorial service. Once they arrived, we were loaded onto two Air Force C-141 Starlifters for the ride home. Although extremely jubilant, we were

Memorial ceremony for Duane Hodges. US Navy photo.

still hesitant to let it all hang out. It was a fast turnaround from terror to being treated like heroes. Some were probably in shock. How
would anyone act under those circumstances?

The planes would have to make a refueling stop before reaching
the continental United States. Landing at Hickam AFB Hawaii was
considered for the refueling location, but the Navy did not want to
take the chance the press or anyone else would be there to interfere.
We landed at Midway Island to refuel before continuing to Miramar
Naval Air Station in San Diego, California.

Once the planes parked at Miramar, we gathered our belongings
and walked in single file toward the waiting crowd. The Navy flew
my parents out to San Diego for the welcome-home celebration. A
large crowd greeted us. A Navy band blared away, news cameras and
reporters were everywhere. We felt like returning heroes!

No reporters were allowed anywhere near us. The first thought on
all of our minds were to meet with our parents and loved ones we

Crew disembarking C-141. Woelk is the one with the bag hanging down the left side of his leg. US Navy photo.

had not seen in well over a year. Needless to say, they were anxiously waiting for our return as well. I had this apprehensive smile on my face, looking over the crowd trying to pick out Mom and Dad. I was still not able to grasp what I was seeing unfold before me.

Luckily, our loved ones were kept away from the news cameras and reporters. We were able to walk right over to where they were all grouped together. I hugged Mom and Dad as Mom cried happy tears not wanting to let go of the moment. We exchanged hugs and kisses, but I did not talk about my prior eleven months, nor did they ask. We were simply glad to be together again!

After everyone had exited the plane, Duane's body was transferred to an ambulance in front of a silent crowd, while taps were played off in the distance. He would soon be making his final trip homeward to be reunited with his family and friends. Duane was buried in a small

Navy pallbearers escorting body of Duane Hodges from aircraft to awaiting hearse. US Navy photo.

pine tree-shaded cemetery, nestled against a hillside on the outskirts of Creswell, Oregon, the town he called home.

I was able to visit Duane's grave many years after my return home. The cemetery could not have been a more appropriate place for my friend to be laid to rest. A rather long, straight, and narrow tree-lined gravel road made its way into the pine tree-shaded cemetery. It was small, very quiet, and secluded from this once booming logging town of Creswell.

Making our way to our loved ones, we hardly noticed the dignitaries and press in attendance. I was still processing what had happened. So much had gone on, not only in the past several hours, but also the recent weeks and the months prior. You can't just flip a switch to take you back to what was normal one year before.

CHAPTER 11
From Hell to Glory

We lost so much of ourselves in those eleven months. None of us will ever fully recover. After our release, we were dealing with flashbacks of beatings, loss of freedom, humiliation, and the probability of the crew answering to the Navy for our actions. Many of the crew thought we were walking to freedom from North Korea only to be incarcerated here in the United States for our actions at sea and in captivity. We were concerned about having signed the confession, no matter how hard we tried to resist. We gave up the ship without firing a single shot, and we were forced to lie about our actual location at sea.

Buses carrying crew to the Balboa Naval Hospital in San Diego. US Navy photo.

Welcome home in San Diego. US Navy photo.

The Navy does not take losing a ship lightly. But at that very minute, we were being treated as heroes from the people of San Diego. After an emotional reunion with loved ones, and all the welcoming home speeches were over at Miramar, we were once again loaded onto buses taking us and our loved ones to our next step in the process.

The streets and highways from Miramar Naval Air Station to Balboa Naval Hospital were closed to local traffic. The roadways were lined with people waving flags and displaying handmade posters to welcome us home.

Again, a lot to process in a very short time from hell to glory; from Pyongyang to San Diego. The buses made their way to where we would be spending the next several weeks. We were put in a barracks within walking distance of the Balboa Naval Hospital in San Diego. Once again, clean sheets, soft bed, nice pillow, no cracks in the floor, the walls were freshly painted, and we did not worry about getting kicked, beaten or harassed anymore. We were put through intense physicals and psychological evaluation to determine our condition, physical and mental well-being.

After being subjected to starvation, physical and mental trauma, one of the first actions was to have blood drawn. After that I remember getting up to walk out the door. Next thing I knew I was being helped up off the floor. Most of the crew were surprisingly doing okay, considering what we had gone through. But before all of the official process to get us back into Navy life could start, it was Christmas, time to spend with our loved ones.

A welcome-home Christmas dinner was prepared for crew, families, some high-ranking officers, and of course the Navy photographers who were capturing the moment. However, these photos would not be used for propaganda, but to record history.

Spending Christmas with loved ones we had not seen for more than a year was indescribable. Unbeknownst to me, my dad made a

Crew treated to a welcome home Christmas dinner at Balboa Naval Hospital. Woelk is located center left, with his back to the camera, his mother to his right. US Navy photo.

Woelk playing his new Gretsch guitar. US Navy photo.

deal with a local music store in San Diego to purchase a new Gretsch Viking guitar. What a surprise Christmas present that was! I never told Dad how much I needed that guitar as a distraction from all that was going on in my life at the time. It allowed me to get lost in my own little world and not worry about what was going to happen next.

Music has always been important to me, including playing in a band when I was young. It was also part of my long-term recovery, as I played guitar in a band for a while ten years after my release. After I retired, I picked up a couple of guitars online and started playing again. Playing the guitar was definitely therapeutic.

One would think this would be an easy adjustment, but it was not. Some were dealing with broken marriages, death of family members, PTSD, and anxiety over how the Navy would treat us for losing the Pueblo and signing those confessions.

We were able to spend 24 December, the day we arrived home, and Christmas Day with our loved ones before they had to leave. The time we had with loved ones was short, once again the up and down roller-coaster ride, then screaming back to reality once again with the medical evaluations at Balboa.

During our time with our families, we still wore the jump suits handed out at Panmunjom upon our release. The time had come for us to be issued brand new Navy duds. Since we were at San Diego, the location of the Naval Training Center, why not run us through the supply depot where uniforms are issued to the new recruits. Just like in boot camp we all formed a line in front of the counter where we were handed our new clothes. Everything we were issued in boot camp was reissued to us on that day. It felt good to have the advancement of 3rd Class Petty Officer rank sewn on my sleeve. The lower ranked were all advanced one step at that time. I was so proud to wear brand new Navy Blues.

There was a lot going on shortly after our release. The Navy conducted physicals to assess our general health. Both the Navy and the NSA interrogated us, to learn about what happened during the attack and in the aftermath. We had to get back into the Navy's routine. We were all receiving numerous cards and letters from family and friends while at the Balboa Hospital. Captain Bucher and the crew received a letter from the Apollo 8 astronauts welcoming us home prior to their landing.

NATIONAL SECURITY AGENCY INTERROGATIONS

We were not allowed to leave the confinements of our barracks at Balboa. We were put through rigorous questioning. Many of the crew, mainly the CTs, thought this was the beginning of being charged for what they did in captivity against the rules. The Navy and the NSA were concerned about what was destroyed and what might have fallen into the hands of North Korea. North Korea was more interested in the ship and crew than what we were carrying.

However, Russia was very much interested in what could be salvaged. The number one item they were really concerned about was the code machine. The CTs had to keep the lines of communication open right up until it was determined we were going to be boarded. When all communication was ended with the Navy or NSA, the CTs attempted to destroy that machine. The Navy had devices that could be used to destroy electronic equipment in a matter of seconds, but Bucher was told it was too expensive and not needed. Sledgehammers and axes were the means provided by the Navy to destroy what we had. From my understanding, the sledges and axes bounce off the equipment causing minimal damage.

I have read in one of the books written after the release of classified documents several years back, the Russians were able to obtain a lot of classified equipment and documents. However, they were missing a key link to make this equipment work. Convicted John Walker, a Navy Chief Warrant Officer, provided Russia with what was needed. But that is another story I do not know enough about to include in this book.

My interrogation went well. My duty on Pueblo had nothing to do with top secret or highly classified documents. However, I was removing highly classified documents from Bucher's personal safe. This safe may or may not have held a very important device used in inscription.

I was asked if I had seen the device he described and, if so, was it destroyed? I had no recollection that the device he was referring to was in the safe when I was removing material.

Since I was the only crewman who was separated from the crew during my hospital stay, my interrogator started asking what I remembered about the jeep ride. I was not able to see much from under the blanket but could hear some things that were going on. I told him the jeep traveled on a gravel road; we stopped at a checkpoint requiring the driver to provide papers.

I told him how long the trip lasted. All the time I was talking, he was shuffling 8 x 10 photos on the table in front of me. When I finished, he showed me a photo of the hospital I was taken to. Another photo he showed me was of the compound where we were being held when released. So, in my opinion, yes there was someone there who knew exactly how we were being treated and where we were at all times.

There was another welcome-home party arranged specifically for the crew, family members who stayed with crewmen, a few dignitaries and a couple of Hollywood stars who wanted to attend and give us a proper welcome. This party was held at a local San Diego hotel. The Navy had us all staying at the hotel because we were not to be in contact with the general public. The order was given not to talk with the press and the press was not allowed anywhere near us.

I had no civilian dress clothes, so I needed to go shopping somewhere. A clothing shop was located near the hotel, making it handy for me to go shopping. I had no idea what to look for in the way of a coat, a tie, pants, and shoes. I relied on the sales clerk, who waited on me to make those decisions. I was a little surprised at what he was about to suggest, but this was southern California. It was a little different than rural Kansas. He brought out a light blue blazer, a "Hi-Tie" instead of a regular tie, ordinary slacks and shoes. I was not sure about the "Hi-Tie"-look for me, so we agreed maybe a clip-on tie would be more appropriate. All decked out, it was time to head for our next welcome-home party.

Captain Bucher started the festivities by cutting a large sheet cake with his officer's sword. One reason for the party was to hand out a

 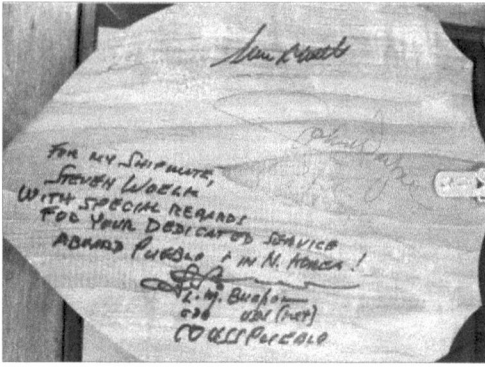

Steven Woelk's personal ship's plaque presented by Captain Bucher. Steven Woelk photo.

USS Pueblo plaque honoring each of us. The plaque had the ship's emblem in a bronze casting with a wood backing.

The celebrities attending the presentation were John Wayne and Pat Boone. John Wayne was my favorite actor of all time, so it was an honor to meet him in person. Pat Boone presented my plaque to me, so it was neat meeting him also. Meeting John Wayne was the highlight of my life at that moment. I asked John Wayne, Pat Boone, and Captain Bucher to sign the back of my Pueblo plaque to capture the moment forever.

BEACH PARTY, CONCERTS AND CELEBRITIES

One of the first things many of us wanted to do after we returned home was to buy a car. I took all the money I had earned in the past year, a little over $4,000, to purchase a used 1967 Mercury Cougar. I do not remember how many miles it had on it, but it had all the bells and whistles. My friends bought brand new cars, a 1969 Mach I Ford Mustang, a Ford Torino and a Ford Fairlane 500, all very impressive cars but out of my class or price range. My friend who bought the

Presentations by John Wayne and Pat Boone. US Navy photos.

Ford Mustang took it to a local shop where he rebuilt the engine to around 500 hp.

Leaving my car at the barracks, the four of us were at some function where we took separate cars. I was with Rich in the Mach 1, when the other two came up beside us indicating they wanted to challenge us. There was no one on the interstate so we decided it was time to compare the speed of the Mach 1 Mustang to the Ford 500. The Fairlane was fast but did not have a chance with the "made to go fast" Mustang. The speedometer was not hooked up on the Mustang, so I asked how fast he thought we were going. I knew we were flying down the interstate but did not realize we were going about 140 mph. I found out several years later he had to sell the Mustang, because every time he would take it out the cops would follow him, waiting for him to take off. A car like that is no fun if you can't open it up once in a while.

A beach party was organized at La Jolla Cove, located up the coast from San Diego. We were told there would be a group of college girls

A very happy Steven Woelk (second from left), singer Andy Williams (middle) and Howard Bland (second from right) at the evening dinner party hosted by Andy Williams. US Navy photo.

from one of the local college dorms there wanting to meet some of the crew. Since we all had wheels and were released from quarantine, we were ready, willing and able to meet some girls. The young lady I met was a student living east of San Diego. We hit it off and dated for the next several weeks until it was time for us to be released and go our separate ways.

The City of San Diego graciously offered so many opportunities to keep us busy while in their city. I took my new girlfriend to nice restaurants, pizza joints, Sea World, the San Diego Zoo, and concerts, all made available to the crew through the generous donations of various organizations and restaurants.

Andy Williams was in town for his annual charity golf tournament and evening gala, where he gave a concert performance. The crew received tickets for anyone who wanted to attend his concert. Three of us took the girls we met on the beach to his show. Decked out in our Navy uniforms, and the girls dressed for the occasion, we were ready for a night out. Time to forget about The Bear and enjoy the good ol' USA!

After the concert our dates went into the restroom to freshen up. While there they met a couple of ladies who invited us all to the after-concert dinner. The dinner was over but the socializing had just started. We all had our pictures taken with Andy Williams and his wife. There was quite a list of popular entertainers in attendance, including Danny Thomas, Alan Hale, and Trini Lopez, to name a few. It was another night to remember.

The entire crew had the opportunity to ride in the Goodyear Blimp while it was in town for an event. They took us over the city of San Diego, then back to the airport. Several of the San Diego Chargers cheerleading squad were there to meet and greet us prior to getting on the blimp. The weather was perfect, so it was a wonderful afternoon to go for a ride.

We attended a Johnny Cash concert while he was touring southern California. Unfortunately, I did not have the opportunity to meet him. Captain Bucher went backstage to meet him. Sadly, I didn't know that he had done that. If I had known beforehand, there is no doubt in my mind the captain would have invited me along with him for the meet and greet. I would have made it known that Cash was my favorite all-time country star, and I would really have liked to meet him.

During a crew reunion years later, Navy Chief James Kell was interviewed by KPBS TV in San Diego. He said that surviving the nearly year-long captivity in North Korea came down to three things, "Faith in God, my country and my Navy. I knew that those three things, if I had those, I was going to be okay. I was determined that they could take my body, but they were never going to get my mind."

CHAPTER 12
Welcome Home Steve!

Crew members who stayed in the Navy were given a choice of their next duty station, within reason. Many of the crew were reservists so they were released from the service after processing. I had one more year to serve, so I decided I would like to go to the Navy's Electrician's Mate School at Great Lakes Naval Base.

Before we were imprisoned, I held the rank of E-3. When we returned, I was advanced to the rank of E-4 as an Electrician's Mate (EM). Before I received orders to go to my next duty station, the Navy advanced me to E-5 with the stipulation that I pass the E-5 test within a year to retain the rank. My request to attend Electrician's Mate school at Great Lakes was approved and I was on my way.

The Navy was about to get me restarted with a bang, but I thought long and hard about what I was getting myself into. I had orders to a school set up for guys right out of boot camp or lower-ranked sailors wanting to become electricians, and I would show up as an E-5 EM with absolutely no experience. Would I really want to do that? I decided to try a different route with the Navy. Asking our Corpsman about the chances of me getting a medical discharge, he assured me I would not have any trouble at all.

I medically retired from the Navy as an E-5 Electrician's Mate, with a low disability rating. I had the option of waiving the Navy retirement/disability and converting to a Veterans Administration Disability, which started out with the better rating of 43 percent.

Rethinking my decision, I should have taken the school, just to get the training. The experience would have given me a boost into the electrical industry after getting out of the service one year later.

One day while I was in the gathering area of the barracks, a Navy photographer came in with an armload of 8 x 10 black and white photos. I was standing by the table when he spread the photos out, telling me to help myself. Rummaging through them I picked the ones that were of me or any I just wanted to have for my own. The black and white Navy photos in this book are from that stack of 8 x 10s.

MY NAVY DISCHARGE

When the dust settled in San Diego, I was on my way home. After leave, it was either off to our next duty station, getting an Honorable Discharge, or, in my case, a Medical Discharge from the Navy. I was the only Pueblo crew member to receive a medical discharge for the wounds received during the North Korean gunboat attack.

After returning to Coronado Island in San Diego for final processing, I was on my own. Other shipmates were either discharged or sent off to their new duty station. Some I would never see again. While waiting for the discharge process, I was bunking with sailors I did not know. I figured I would only be there for a few days and then head back home. I do not remember how long I waited for the discharge to be finalized, but it was long enough for someone to think a Second-Class Petty Officer should be on duty doing something. They soon learned of my reason for being there and left me alone during the rest of my stay.

One day, while getting ready to leave the barracks, I heard the steel lockers rattling next to me on the second floor where my bunk was located. Before I could determine what was making the racket the entire building started swaying back and forth.

EARTHQUAKE!

It was a minor quake, causing minimal damage around San Diego. As a Kansas boy, I was used to tornados, where you can go to a cellar or basement to get out of its destructive path. Earthquakes give you no warning and very little protection from their devastation. I would choose a twister over shaky ground.

It was never my intention to stay in the Navy. I was not cut out for a military career. I had done my duty, served honorably and suffered a pretty severe hit for my country. I felt it was time to head back to Kansas and get on with the next phase of my life.

My brother Jon came out to San Diego the week before I was due to go home. I wanted to get back to Kansas as soon as possible, so we took turns driving straight through. The next morning, after we arrived home in Alta Vista, Dad drove me down Main Street for the first time after being away for a year and a half. Halfway down Main Street, high above the ground in the air stretched a "Welcome Home Steve" banner, compliments of my hometown.

A dinner was set up for me one evening at the old lunchroom where I attended school. Many of my high school and family friends were present. The food was served by the same staff who served me back when I was in high school, before I became an unwilling celebrity.

I enjoyed small get-togethers, but at some point, all of the welcome-home festivities came to an end. Alta Vista is one of those small, Midwestern towns where most people knew each other, and many would gossip about each other or gripe about something else.

You cannot rely on the news to keep you up on current events in a small town without gossip. There's an old saying, "tell Mary or telephone" to get the word out. I miss the people I knew back then, but most of them have passed on, replaced by a newer, much younger generation, who do things differently than we did.

Dad was excited that I was safe, home and ready to start living again. Prior to me arriving home, he had been talking with a local car dealership about a new 1969, 383 hp Dodge Charger. Having already bought a nice used car in San Diego that was paid for, I was not wanting to get into debt starting out. What harm would it cause if I took a look at the car? That was the wrong thing to do, I loved the car. I talked to the local banker about a loan and like most people young and eager, I started my new life in debt. But I really liked that car.

There was a local mechanic from the area with the reputation of being top-notch. He was into fast muscle cars. He drove a 454 hp Chevy Chevelle, known to car enthusiasts for miles around. Just outside of town was a quarter-mile stretch of highway with a start and finish line painted on the blacktop. He would challenge guys to race, because he knew he could beat just about anyone around.

He kept badgering me to race, but I was not into that. I knew he was not going to leave me alone until I accepted his challenge, so I agreed to meet him out at the starting line. We lined up, someone counted down, tires lit up, and down the two-lane road we went. I was ahead of him off the line but he came up fast. It was close, but I smoked his ass by a bumper at the finish line.

The badgering started all over again and he wanted a rematch. I wasn't interested. I got the racing title. I was good with that, I never raced anyone again.

I was driving back to my parents' house one afternoon when I saw one of my high school teachers sitting on his front porch. He had retired shortly before that, so I stopped, and we chatted for nearly an hour. I never dreamed I would ever sit down with this man to shoot the bull. Mr. Bonar was well-respected in the community. He had taught in Alta Vista for decades and in his younger days coached all the sports offered in our small school.

Mr. Bonar taught the algebra class that took me two years to finally pass. Although at the time I did not understand the importance of taking the course, later I realized it would be needed to understand the theory of electricity. When I was a senior in high school, several of us decided to celebrate our eigtheenth birthdays, the legal drinking age in Kansas, by skipping school. Scotty, who was also one of my Navy buddies, and I, called in sick that day. Why we drove so far to have our first drink in a bar I do not remember. We headed for Topeka, an hour away, to order a beer. Somehow Mr. Bonar, superintendent of the Alta Vista High School at the time, found out about our endeavor. He nearly suspended us, but instead began chewing us out for what we did.

I was not in any hurry to go anywhere so I stopped, walked up to where he was sitting and sat down beside him. That was the first time I had a serious talk with him away from school. We talked about anything and everything, except my past education disaster or what happened to me in North Korea.

My health after returning home, with a few minor issues, was pretty good. When I had surgery in North Korea the doctor did not suture my wounds properly, so I had to have it corrected at the VA Hospital in Topeka. It was a minor repair, but I had to stay in the hospital for a couple of days.

What was different about this particular surgery was the stainless steel sutures used to sew me up. The exposed wire ends were very sharp and they would not give at all whenever I moved, which was very painful. Stainless steel sutures were common practice for that particular type of surgery back in those days. Stainless steel was less likely to get infected when they had to be left in longer than the traditional sutures. The kite string used on me in North Korea would have been a better choice, I think.

THOUGHTS ABOUT A HERO'S WELCOME

The hero's welcome I received upon returning home felt undeserved. True heroes, in my eyes, were those who stare down danger on the battlefield, who willingly risk their lives to save others. My experience, while harrowing, wasn't one of direct combat. But war isn't just about front lines; it's a complex web where every role plays a vital part. Following orders to destroy sensitive documents during that brutal assault on the Pueblo was my contribution, however small it may seem in the grand scheme of things.

We were thrust into a situation where our actions could have a ripple effect, impacting the broader conflict. And while I have the invisible wounds of captivity, the nightmares and the constant state of alert are my constant reminder of the price of service.

The men and women who serve our country, in whatever capacity, deserve our deepest respect and gratitude. They endure hardship, face danger, and carry the weight of their experiences long after the battles are over. They are the true heroes, the ones who embody the courage, the selflessness, and the unwavering dedication that defines what it means to serve a cause greater than oneself.

The Pueblo Incident is often overshadowed by other events of 1968. Unlike the Tet Offensive, a brutal frontline battle, ours was a different kind of fight. It was a fight for survival in the face of an unexpected attack, a fight to maintain order and protect our fellow crewmates during a harrowing eleven-month captivity. Captain Bucher's courageous decision to destroy sensitive documents, a split-second choice under fire, stands as a testament to his leadership and his unwavering commitment to the safety of his men.

The crew's resilience during captivity is a story of unwavering determination, of the human spirit's ability to endure unimaginable hardship. Our ordeal deserves to be remembered, not relegated to the footnotes of history.

Let the Pueblo Incident serve as a reminder of the sacrifices made by all those who serve our country, in the face of danger on the battlefield or in the quiet courage displayed during captivity. Let us honor their stories, learn from their experiences, and ensure that this piece of history never fades from memory.

Epilogue

The past decades have been very good to me. I have had the privilege to do things many never have a chance to experience. Having exceptional parents helped me to mature as a man, even before I entered the Navy. Being able to talk about my experience on the Pueblo has never been an issue with me. I never talked about it during my working years because no one asked me about it.

I have hunted pheasant, quail, ducks, dove, deer, fished farm ponds and lakes in the Midwest all the way to Canada. I never claimed to be good at hunting or fishing but I sure enjoyed having the opportunity.

School was not easy for me through all twelve years. Never considered going to college due to my poor grades and unwillingness to study.

I have had good work ethics ever since I was old enough to get a job. Always felt the need to work, make a living, saving to buy what I could afford or support a family.

I have been present in the delivery room with two of our kids, cutting the umbilical cord on our son, welcoming him into life.

Participating in so many veterans' events after my retirement from the COE. Meeting some remarkable former WWII Prisoners of War being a member of the American Ex-Prisoner of War organization. The stories they told, the lives they led after their release. This is the only organization I felt comfortable with. The Pueblo fell between the cracks in the VFW and American Legion. I was a Vietnam-era vet, not a Vietnam Vet. I did not feel I had anything in common with its members. I was never on that battlefield. Yes, I was wounded by enemy fire, but to me that is different from being at war day after day.

I'm not the type of person to start a conversation about my military days. My conversations about the Pueblo usually start with someone else asking about my Pueblo cap.

Accepting speaking events for various organizations around the Kansas City area has allowed me to get my story out. My injuries have been written about in nearly every book released about the USS Pueblo. I co-authored *The Last Voyage of the USS Pueblo* shortly after returning home. A couple of films about us have been produced over the years. The first being a play for television, *Pueblo* in 1973, and the second film was by Bill Lowe called *Pueblo-A Year of Crisis in America*. The DVD has not been released to the public but is being shown for private events.

One of the most memorable events I was privileged to be a part of was the Kansas City Heartland Honor Flight in 2024. Not only did I spend the day with 90 heroes, I was asked to join three Vietnam veterans in a wreath ceremony at the Tomb of the Unknown Soldier. What an honor for me, WOW! How in the world do you top that?

I assume the Honor Flight event organizers all over the United States do a remarkable job setting them up. The Heartland Honor Flight organizers went way beyond what is expected of them. The day went great going to all of the scheduled stops, the major monuments. We did have a problem getting on the plane at the airport. The plane was half loaded when no one else was allowed to board. Then after about thirty minutes, we were removed from the plane. Apparently, an air conditioning problem put a hold on our departure. About forty-five minutes later we were allowed back onto the plane, and ready to go. After sitting for another forty-five minutes on the plane we were told to deplane once again. This plane was not going back to Kansas City on that day. Now this is where the Kansas City Honor Flight team went into action. Getting closer to midnight, a trip to the 5-star hotel was arranged and we all took an Uber to the hotel for the night. The next morning, we had transportation to the airport and a plane in waiting. We were allowed to board on time, letters from home were handed out, tears flowed as we read the pages. We landed on time and walked between two lines of cheering family and friends. Although it was a delay of nearly 12 hours, it was an experience to remember. Grateful thanks to the Heartland Honor Flight Team of Kansas City.

Now I know there is always a plan B for various reasons. A plane grounded for whatever reason is not an easy problem to correct. A correction may not have run smoothly but when you have an Honor Flight crew like we had, no problem, they have their act together. I have been so blessed to live long enough to take part in some remarkable experiences and to live in a country where now veterans are honored. The Vietnam Vets are finally getting the Welcome Home they justly deserve, but is long overdue.

(Don Bolkan, Steven Woelk, Cecil Hoffman, John Folk)

There are so many people in my life who have influenced the way I have turned out in one way or another. The night before my two friends and I left for the Navy, we played our last dance together at the Pearl Theater in Alta Vista. Through all the years I played in future bands, Cecil Hoffman was the best drummer I would ever have the pleasure of playing in front of. We all got along very well, having fun at every event, and never argued about anything.

The guys I met going into the service, bootcamp recruits and in Bremerton prior to getting my sea legs were all good friends. Those who I roomed with in North Korea helped me get through some very tough mentally and physically trying times. The men and women I had the privilege of working with after leaving the military were truly special. My Pastor helped me through the years, not only on a personal level but his woodworking projects helped me deal with PTSD. Those individuals who donate their time and money to provide once-in-a-lifetime events for me. The authors of the books who wrote about the Pueblo Incident placing the blame where it should have been.

I cannot say enough about my family. Kathy has stuck with me through the many years when I thought what I was experiencing was normal. Our daughter touched our lives so much even though she was only with us for a short time. Our son is a wonderful husband and terrific father to his two children.

None of this would have turned out the way it did if not for my sacred belief in God. I am so blessed to have become a Christian at a young age. Although I was not a churchgoer, or had a deep understanding of the Bible, my prayers helped me deal with virtually all of what was troubling me at the time. I never prayed for miracles but for the ability to cope with whatever was going on. Life is never easy but can be softened through prayer.

REVIEWS

Pig Fat Soup is an astonishing revelation of bravery and resilience by the crew of the spy ship USS Pueblo, seized in international waters by North Korea, and their eleven months of torture and near starvation as POWs. A must-read for anyone suffering emotional distress!

Bryce F Lockwood, USMC
Only Marine Survivor, USS Liberty

This is the incredible account of a young man from Kansas, Steven Woelk. After high school, he joined the US Navy and was assigned to the ship USS Pueblo. The Pueblo was captured by a Communist nation while performing its assigned duty.

The capture of the Pueblo by a hostile nation is certainly a significant event in history and should never be forgotten. During his capture, Woelk endured barbaric medical treatment for his numerous wounds, relentless interrogations, beatings and a primitive diet. His faith and love of family and country kept him going during this period of psychological hell.

This is a story of his successful return to civilian life and how he copes with everyday life. I am in awe of my friend, Steven Woelk, and I'm elated he is telling his compelling story.

CWO-5 Walt Schley, USMC (Ret)

Pig Fat Soup is a testament to the inner strength of a Kansas boy, thrust into the sudden horrors of becoming a POW of an inhumane regime. Steven Woelk's compelling story is not only of the brutality of his captors and the bond that developed between his fellow shipmates, but of the failures of the U.S. Navy, which put the USS Pueblo in jeopardy even before its mission off the North Korean coast.

Lt. Col. (Ret) Greg Shuey, U.S. Air Force

Pig Fat Soup is a well-written, detailed story of the great sacrifice, suffering and endurance of the sailors of the captured USS Pueblo in January 1968 by the North Koreans. Captured in international waters, they were confined as prisoners of war until released in December 1968.

Steve's book gives a view of character development as a small-town youth who sustained those difficult months of capture. His description of the incarceration gives an inside view of the torture and emotional trauma he suffered during those difficult times, trauma that remains for his entire life.

Lane Smith, Buck Sergeant E-5
U.S. Army, Vietnam Veteran

Steve walks his talk as his life has been one of service to his family, God, and country. From the time he left his Kansas community to serve in the Navy he was filled with a trepidation for what was coming and a bravado to meet it head on. His journey took him to a place that few have known, a prison in North Korea. He lived in that locked down POW world for eleven months. The readers of Pig Fat Soup will gain a deep appreciation and understanding about what the Pueblo crew was experiencing during those months of terror. Thankfully, Steve lets his readers decompress and takes them back with him to the USA, experiencing a hero's welcome home. He then gives them a look at life after the celebrations have ended. He has quietly made a living and raised his family.

Mel Carney, 1LT, US Army, Americal Division,
Chu Lai Defense Command

In 1968 most of America and nations throughout the world, were focused on American involvement in Vietnam. Approximately 1,500 miles from South Vietnam, in the Sea of Japan, a situation was developing that would be forever etched in the annals of U.S. Naval History. The USS Pueblo was attacked and seized by the North Korean military. Steven Woelk was severely wounded during this attack. This is his story; how and why he was there; how the crew was constantly tortured; medical operations without any anesthesia; the hundreds of intelligence documents aboard the Pueblo that were not destroyed before the North Koreans took over the ship. This book gives the reader not only an in-depth, personal account of the eleven-month incarceration of the crew but also speaks to the unpreparedness of the ship, lack of foresight by the Department of the Navy and US Government. PIG FAT SOUP gives you the detailed, chilling, personal experience of this prisoner of war.

Kris Harris, NCOIC USMC, 3rd Marine Amphibious Force, Combat Information Bureau, Combat Reporter Unit

Bibliography

1. Bamford, James (2001). Body of Secrets. Doubleday. ISBN 0099427745.

2. Ennes, James M. Jr (1987). Assault on the Liberty: The True Story of the Israeli Attack on an American Intelligence Ship. New York: Random House. ISBN 978-5-87232-402-7.; ussliberty.org Archived 9 March 2022 at the Wayback Machine

3. Gerhard, William D.; Millington, Henry W. (1981). Attack on a SIGINT Collector, the USS Liberty (PDF). NSA History Report, U.S. Cryptologic History series (Report). National Security Agency. Archived from the original (PDF) on 30 October 2012. partially declassified 1999, 2003.

4. The Attack on the 'Liberty' Incident (PDF) (Report). Israel Defence Forces, History Department. June 1982.

5. Colonel Ram Ron (16 June 1967). Ram Ron Report (PDF) (Report). Israel Defense Forces Inquiry Commission Report.

6. Lenczowski, George (1990). American presidents and the Middle East. Duke University Press. ISBN 978-0-8223-0963-5.

7. Oren, Michael B. (Spring 2000). "The USS Liberty: Case Closed."

8. Scott, James (2009). The Attack on the Liberty: The Untold Story of Israel's Deadly 1967 Assault on a U.S. Spy Ship. Simon & Schuster. ISBN 978-1-4165-5482-0.

9. "The Special Project Fleet". coldwar-c4i.net. Archived from the original on 2015-09-06.

10. "AGER_Program". www.usspueblo.org. Archived from the original on 2015-10-25.

11. ^ Newton, Robert E. (1992). "The Capture of the USS Pueblo and Its Effect on SIGINT Operations" (PDF). U.S. Cryptologic History, Special Series, Crisis Collection, Vol. 7, National Security Agency (NSA). pp. 9–18. Archived (PDF) from the original on 5 January 2019. Retrieved 4 January 2019.

12. "Wikimapia.org Tag". Archived from the original on 14 December 2006. Retrieved 17 June 2010.

13. Gerhard, William D.; Millington, Henry W. (1981). Attack on a SIGINT Collector, the USS Liberty (PDF). NSA History Report, U.S. Cryptologic History series (Report). National Security Agency. Archived from the original (PDF) on 30 October 2012. partially declassified 1999, 2003.

14. Cristol, A.Jay (2013). The Liberty Incident Revealed: The Definitive Account of the 1967 Israeli Attack on the U.S. Navy Spy Ship. Naval Institute Press. pp. 61, 113–114. ISBN 978-1-61251-387-4.

15. Findings of Fact, Opinions, and Recommendations of a Court of Inquiry Convened by Order of Commander in Chief, United States Pacific Fleet, to Inquire into the Circumstances Relating to the Seizure of USS Pueblo (AGER-2).

16. Lloyd M. Bucher and Mark Rascovich, Bucher: My Story (New York: Doubleday & Co., 1970).

17. Karen L. Gatz, ed., Foreign Relations of the United States, 1964–1968, Vol. XXIX, Part 1, Korea, (U.S. Government Printing Office, Washington, D.C., 2000).

18. National Security File, Country File, Korea, box 57, folder: *Pueblo* Incident, vol. 1a, part A, Lyndon B. Johnson Library.

19. Tom Johnson's Notes of Meetings, 24 January 1968, 1 p.m., *Pueblo* II, National Security Council, container no. 2, Lyndon B. Johnson Library.

20. Details of the Naval Investigative Service probe of Bucher are contained in multiple documents located at the National Archives, Record Group 526, Records of the Naval Criminal Investigative Service, US6500, 26–27 January 1968, box 13.

21. National Security File, National Security Council Histories, *Pueblo* Crisis 1968, vol. 4, Day by Day Documents, Part 5, box 28, Lyndon B. Johnson Library. The author obtained a partially redacted copy of the CIA profile of Bucher through the Freedom of Information Act.

22. Multiple examples of torture and other abuse of *Pueblo* sailors are described in Bucher Rascovich, *Bucher: My Story and Trevor Armbrister, A Matter of Accountability: The True Story of the Pueblo Affair* (Coward-McCann, New York, 1970).

23. National Security File, Memos to the President—Walt Rostow, vol. 78, 20–24 1968 (2 of 2), box 34, Lyndon B. Johnson Library.

24. Record of Proceedings of a Court of Inquiry, Convened by Order of Commander in Chief, United States Pacific Fleet, to Inquire into the Circumstances Relating to the Seizure of the USS *Pueblo* (AGER-2) by North Korean Naval Forces Which Occurred in the Sea of Japan on 23 January 1968.

Appendix A

AWARDS PRESENTED TO THE PUEBLO CREW

I received several medals for my service aboard the USS Pueblo. The Purple Heart with one gold star (one for being wounded, one for being a POW). The Navy Commendation Medal with gold star and V for valor device counts three total. The Prisoner of War medal, Combat Action Ribbon, Armed Forces Expeditionary and the National Defense medal were all awarded for that brief time of terror in my life.

Captain Bucher recommended Charlie, Bob and me for the Bronze Star for our participation in the destruction of classified documents under enemy fire. Bob was awarded his Bronze Star by the Marine Corps with no questions asked. The Navy decided to lower the award for Charlie and me to the Navy Commendation medal. Everyone on

Last photo taken of the entire crew at Coronado Island across the Bay from San Diego. US Navy photo.

board was awarded the Navy Commendation medal with the "V" for Valor device.

The highest medal awarded to any of our crewmen was the Navy Cross, given to Bob Hammond.

Duane Hodges was awarded the Silver Star posthumously. Captain Bucher presented the medal to Duane's parents in their hometown of Creswell, Oregon.

Most of the crew did not receive medals recommended by Captain Bucher. The Prisoner of War medal was not authorized for us after we had returned home. I was at the VA receiving care when I questioned my doctor about an ailment I thought would be service connected since I was a POW. He said "it is not documented in your record that you were a former POW."

Looking into this further I found out the crew was considered "detainees" by the US government and the Navy, not Prisoners of War. Thinking this is not right since a peace agreement had never been signed with North Korea, I contacted my State Representative Jim Slattery about my concern. He and a couple other politicians introduced legislation to acknowledge we should be designated as POWs. Finally in April 1990 we were considered Former Prisoners of War and were eligible to receive the medal with all the medical benefits that come with the title. A large ceremony was organized in San Diego for the crew to have the medal pinned on our chests. Most all of the crew showed up for the presentation, it was quite an honor.

Although most of us did not get the recognition suggested by Captain Bucher, at least what we did receive is honorable.

Woelk receiving his Purple Heart Medal presentation. US Navy photo.

Commander Bucher receiving his Purple Heart Medal. US Navy photo.

USS Pueblo
Prisoner of War Medal
Presentation
May 5, 1990
County Administration Center
San Diego, California

USS Pueblo Prisoner of War Medal Presentation. May 8 1990, County Administration Center, San Diego, California. US Navy photo.

Medals and ribbons, left to right: Purple Heart with Gold Star, indicates two awards in text we mentioned he was awarded one for being wounded and the second was awarded to all crewmen for the torture they endured over 11 months, next is the Navy Combat Action Ribbon, and then the Armed Forces Expeditionary medal. The lower row shows a Navy Commendation medal with "V" for Valor and Gold Star, Prisoner of War medal and then the National Defense Service medal. Steven Woelk photo.

Appendix B

PERIPHERAL MATERIALS

PUBLISHED PUEBLO STORIES

Due to the publicity, public awareness and post-incident fallout, there have been many books written about the events surrounding the Pueblo seizure. Some are good, some are not so good. Although I'm grateful that you are reading my personal story, a short list of others which have been quoted in this book, follows:

- *The Last Voyage of the USS Pueblo*, which I co-authored with 14 fellow crewmen, written by Ed Brandt
- *Bucher My Story*, an autobiography by the ship's commander, Lloyd Bucher
- *The Capture of the USS Pueblo* by James Duermeyer
- *Act of War* by Jack Cheevers
- *Flash Point North Korea, The Pueblo and EC-121 Crisis* by Richard Mobley
- *The Pueblo Incident* by Mitchell Lerner

PATRIOT FEATURES DOCUMENTARY

A nonprofit organization in Kansas City, called "Patriot Features," reached out to me to tell my story in a fifteen-minute audio/visual recording. I continue to present my story throughout the Kansas City area, and share this video in the process. With this video anyone can access my story.

The Patriot Features website contains numerous documentaries of U.S. military veterans who have graciously shared their stories. These can be viewed on *www.Patriotfeatures.org*.

VETERANS ORGANIZATIONS

The Foundation for Exceptional Warriors "The FEW"

When we moved to east central Kansas my hunting opportunities became more difficult. I did not know anyone who owned land that allowed hunting to strangers. I owned several fishing boats over the years that allowed me to fish several local lakes so I focused on fishing.

One day while I was sighting in my rifle at a local range, a gentleman noticed my Purple Heart hat. He handed me a business card suggesting I check out the organization on the front. The website was for the "Foundation for Exceptional Warriors." The FEW accepts applicants who are Purple Heart recipients, "V" for valor recipients, former Prisoners of War, and anyone who was in Special Operations. Ronnie Sweger is the co-founder and executive director of the FEW. Ronnie, an Army Special Forces veteran, one of my heroes, let me know of certain hunting events the FEW provided. I applied and was accepted to participate in several events, a turkey hunt in Missouri, deer hunt in Michigan, fishing on the Hudson River and a Red Stag hunt in Canada. These events are made available through event donors, guides and lodge owners.

Foundation for Exceptional Warriors: *exceptionalwarriors.org*

WOUNDED WARRIORS IN ACTION FOUNDATION

My first events were sponsored by the Wounded Warriors in Action Foundation (WWIAF) and funded by gracious donors from across the United States.

I applied for and was accepted to salmon fish in Washington state, the MO/KAN catfish event on the Missouri River, a duck hunt in the bootheel of Missouri, and the world class MO/KAN Bucks and Ducks hunt in Northwest Missouri.

Wounded Warriors in Action Foundation: *wwiaf.org*

FREEDOM HUNTERS

I was fortunate to attend several events with the foundation Freedom Hunters in Colorado. The first event was a deer hunt in western Kansas around Oakley.

The Jim Shockey Classic Military Charity Event and auction is held annually to support the Freedom Hunters events for veterans throughout the year. I attended the 2021 fundraiser held in Charleston, South Carolina, staying in a multi-bedroom house with the Freedom Fighters founder, the event auctioneer, a couple from western Kansas and a Navy Seal.

At the live auction event, a drawing was held for a three-day trophy trout trip and quail hunt in northern Georgia. You had to be a veteran for your name to be put into the drawing. I did not have the winning raffle ticket but the auctioneer for the event did.

He looked at me then told the audience he was donating this fishing trip and quail hunt to me. I was in total shock by his generosity. The last time I had fished for trout or hunted quail was with my brother twenty-six years prior.

The following year, I received an email from Freedom Hunters event organizer asking if I would be interested in a goose hunt in central Illinois. Since I had never been goose hunting, I told him I was very interested, send me the details. He asked if I had a veteran buddy who would be interested in coming with me as company for the 7-hour trip. A friend of mine from high school, a fellow Navy Vet, agreed to share the weekend hunting experience with me.

Freedom Hunters: *freedomhunters.org*

THE FOUNDATIONS THAT MAKE DREAMS
COME TRUE

The foundations that organize these events do have minimum requirements for the veterans to be eligible. One requires you to have been awarded the Purple Heart.

The FEW broadens those requirements to Purple Heart, Prisoner of War, Special Ops, or having been awarded a ribbon with the Valor designation. The Freedom Hunters, WWIAF and The Foundation for Exceptional Warriors (FEW) are the three organizations that made my hunting and fishing dreams come true.

Appendix C

ANDERSONVILLE, GEORGIA, NATIONAL PRISONER OF WAR MUSEUM

The crew of the Pueblo was invited to the National Prisoner of War Museum in Andersonville, Georgia, to dedicate plaques in honor of Captain Bucher and the crew of the Pueblo. When we were released from North Korea, I kept the clothes I wore crossing the bridge to freedom. They were kept for many years in our basement packed neatly away with the rest of my memorabilia from that year in my life.

The Andersonville Civil War POW Museum did not have anything to represent the USS Pueblo. I contacted the curator to see if they were interested in what I had to offer. I told them what my collection of memorabilia consisted of, and I would be willing to donate it all to the museum.

They were very interested but suggested I either ship it to them or they would eventually have someone in the area to pick it up at our home. It was far too valuable to me and irreplaceable to mail or ship anywhere. Not knowing how long it would take for them to come to pick it up, I decided to deliver it in person. I donated my clothes, the letters I had sent home to my parents, a pack of Kalmaegi cigarettes I smuggled out of North Korea and boxes of newspaper articles my mom had collected when we were in captivity.

Although it is not on permanent display, it is brought out on special occasions throughout the year. The letters and paper clippings are in the Museum Library Archives for anyone who wishes to research what I donated.

Several years later I met a fellow Purple Heart recipient at a recognition ceremony in Lubbock, Texas. He saw my USS Pueblo hat, so he introduced himself to me and said, "I have an 8mm film taken of the Pueblo crew crossing the Bridge of No Return. Would you be interested in it?"

I do not remember ever seeing a movie clip of our release filmed by the Navy or anyone else. Apparently, this short clip was shot by the Swiss liaison who were part of the negotiating team for our release. I thought this definitely needed to be preserved. Once again, I contacted Andersonville who accepted it as part of the Pueblo collection.

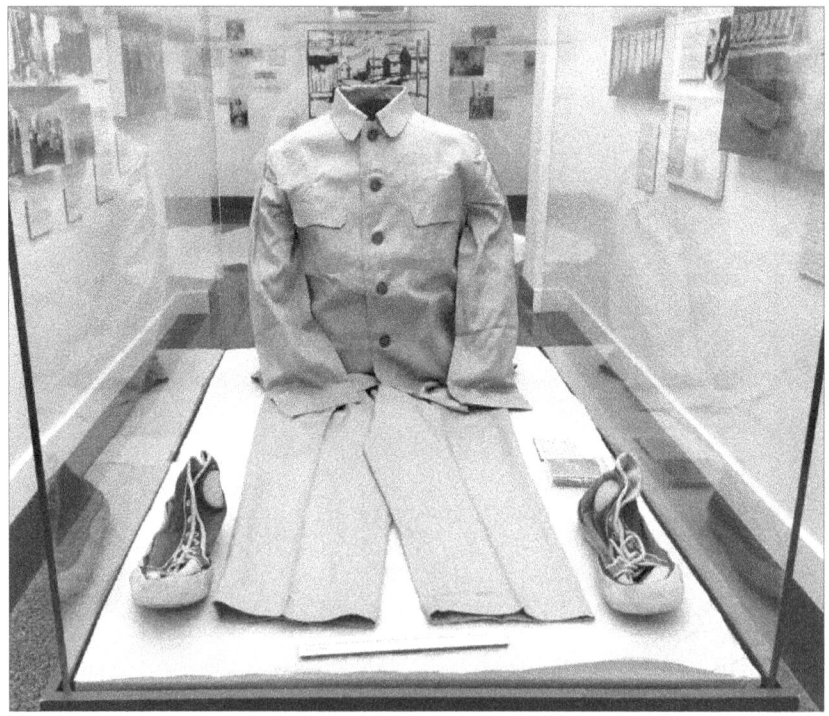

Woelk's prisoner of war clothes on display at the Andersonville, Georgia POW Museum. Photo credit Steven Woelk.

Appendix D

WHERE IS THE USS PUEBLO TODAY?

The USS Pueblo is permanently docked on the Potong River running through Pyongyang, North Korea. It has been moved to several locations within the Pyongyang River system since it was seized in international waters in 1968.

Pueblo dockside in Pyongyang, North Korea. North Korean photo.

The North Koreans have used it as a propaganda museum, telling their one-sided story of what happened on 23 January, 1968, seizing the USS Pueblo. Over the years, there have been some very interesting photos taken aboard the Pueblo. Many were posted on the internet by foreign tourists who went aboard her while they were in North Korea.

The two oldest United States Navy ships still commissioned are the USS Constitution, docked in Boston, Massachusetts, and the USS Pueblo. The Constitution is the oldest and derives its bloodline from the Revolutionary War in the 18th Century, never losing a battle. The Pueblo cannot be decommissioned until it is either returned to the United States or the US flag has been returned.

STILL UNDER FIRE

There are several books criticizing Captain Bucher for giving up the ship without a fight, saying he should have been court-marshaled. There are many more books defending his actions considering the circumstances.

All I have to say about those who criticize his decision at the time, you had to have been there. Don't judge his actions when you have no idea what it was like, what we were up against and what the Navy did or not do to aid in our defense. Eighty-two crewmen were

During the 1969 Navy Court of Inquiry into the North Korean capture of the USS Pueblo, Miles Harvey (left) ably defended the ship's Captain, Commander Lloyd Bucher (right). US Navy photo.

saved by Captain Bucher's decision on 23 January, 1968. We were ill-equipped, outgunned, outnumbered, and without adequate support from the Navy. We did our best to evade the North Koreans, and destroy classified documents and equipment with what was provided by the Navy. The thought of scuttling Pueblo was considered, but the process probably would have taken too long for her to sink. Plus, the Korean gunboats were closing fast with their shells ripping into Pueblo's skin. Even if we would have been able to fight back, the outcome would have been the same. The crew would have been erased.

Over the years, a few individuals have come up to me saying Captain Bucher was wrong for giving up the ship. I look at them and say, "You should have been there, my friend." No matter how I would try to explain the situation there was nothing I could say to convince them any differently. The Navy is set on not giving up the ship without a fight, no exception. But the Navy put us out there under impossible circumstances.

The Navy never provided protection for the Banner Class ships, (Pueblo, Banner and Palm Beach) because nothing serious ever happened during the USS Banner missions. These crews were harassed in international waters on several occasions, but nothing led to what was considered a critical situation until the morning of 23 January 1968, when North Korea committed acts of piracy in the Sea of Japan.

The Navy should have taken the "What If" factor into account. How would the crew of these ships be able to avoid their adversary? How would they defend the ship when attacked? And how would they destroy its highly classified cargo.

At the very least put a Navy submarine out there to show itself when trouble was looming. In our case, the Navy did not take any responsibility for sending us out unprepared. Instead of saying they screwed up, the Navy decided to go after our Captain, cover their mistakes and take him down. Problem solved, or so they thought.

From his autobiographical book, *My Story: Bucher, Lloyd M*, in a chapter entitled, "Don't Start A War Out There, Captain," Admiral Johnson said, "Remember, you're not going out there to start a war, Captain. Make sure you keep them (.50-caliber machine guns) covered and don't use them in any provocative way at all. It doesn't take much to set those damned communists off and start an international incident. That's the last thing we want!"

Bucher was not found guilty of any indiscretions and continued his Navy career until retirement at the rank of commander. In 1989, the U.S. government finally recognized the crew's sacrifice and granted prisoner-of-war medals. No American military operations have been attempted to retrieve USS Pueblo. The ship is officially carried as a commissioned ship in the United States Navy's Naval Vessel Register. It remains captive in North Korea as a tourist attraction and propaganda tool.

ACKNOWLEDGEMENTS

I would like to extend a special thank you to everyone who influenced my life or worked with me on this venture.

First and foremost, thank you Heavenly Father for Your guidance throughout my time here on Earth.

Thank you to my family, who did not give up on me when I thought my anxiety was normal. Thank you to Richard, Scotty, Terry, Jim and numerous friends I had growing up and living in a small town.

Thank you to Duane Hodges, my friend, who made the ultimate sacrifice.

Thank you to Pastor Weinkauf, my pastor and a friend.

Thank you to Bob Chicca for being there in captivity when I needed assurance. And thank you to my roomies in captivity for keeping our spirits alive.

Thank you to Richard DeRosset for the painting he provided for the cover of this book. A painting that was created exclusively for this book.

Thank you to Mel Carney, who convinced me I needed to write about my experience.

Thank you to my veteran friends I have coffee with every week. Thank you to Ronny with the Foundation for Exceptional Warriors; Anthony with Freedom Hunters; and Brian, his gang and the Napier Hunting Lodge with the Wounded Warriors in Action Foundation, for making my hunting and fishing dreams come true.

Thank you to Storyteller Publishing for helping me get my book published. Thank you especially to Rob Lofthouse for his tireless work in taking my thoughts and making them flow.

I am so blessed to know all of these people and have them as a part of my life from the beginning. Without them my life may have gone in a totally different direction.

Steven Woelk

PERSONAL APPEAL

Growing up in a small Midwestern town felt like living in a Norman Rockwell painting. Everyone knew your name, and neighbors were like extended family. My parents were always there for me, supporting me, nurturing me and teaching me right from wrong. Maybe it was because everything felt so secure, or maybe it was just teenage rebellion, but I took their love and support for granted.

In the years that followed, I met some truly remarkable people who left a lasting impact on my life. During my time in the Navy, First Class Petty Officer Blansett, and Third Class Petty Officer Darrell Wright were the two that gave me direct orders. Darrell and several of us from the engine room went out together in the evenings. They also became mentors, teaching me valuable leadership skills and the importance of discipline. In my church community, I found a network of friends who offered unwavering support through thick and thin, celebrating my successes and offering a shoulder to cry on during challenges. Overall, I've been incredibly fortunate to have such a supportive network throughout my life. These people have helped me grow, challenged me to be my best self, and most importantly, shown me the true meaning of friendship.

Back when I was growing up, corporal punishment was a fact of life. When my brother and I got a taste of the leather strap, it usually meant we'd done something wrong, like ditching school or sneaking out after curfew. While it stung at the time, I never felt like my parents were cruel or abusive but just trying to raise us right, the way they were raised.

I only knew my mom's side of the family growing up, although she was adopted as a baby. My dad's parents passed away before I was born. Mom's adopted parents, Grandma and Grandpa Ratliff, lived a few hours away, so visits were infrequent. Grandma, a Swedish immigrant who arrived with her parents in the late 1800s, spoke with a thick accent and baked the most incredible cinnamon rolls. Grandpa, a skilled carpenter, was always busy with projects around the community. I remember the warmth of his workshop, the comforting smell of sawdust, and the way his hands seemed to dance with the wood.

My brother Jon and I weren't exactly close growing up. Like ships passing in the night, he had his friends, and I had mine. But something shifted as we entered middle age. Maybe it was the sobering reality of time, or maybe just a shared yearning for connection. Whatever the reason, we started doing things together like taking hunting and fishing trips to reconnect. It wasn't always easy rebuilding the relationship, but we had a newfound appreciation for each other's company.

Just as we were starting to enjoy each other's company, I received a phone call at work that turned my world upside down. "Jon had a brain aneurysm," the nurse said. My brother was in the ICU at a Wichita hospital, three hours away. My stomach lurched. Fear, cold and sharp, clawed its way up my throat. I raced home, threw some clothes in a bag, and hit the road. While driving down the interstate highway, thoughts of Jon's laughter were crowded out by a terrifying vision of him hooked up to machines, fighting for his life. When I finally reached the hospital and saw his wife with tears of desperation streaming down her face, the weight of the situation crashed over me.

Jon's anticipated recovery would be a long, arduous journey. The once vibrant man who loved sports, fishing and hunting was now struggling to relearn basic tasks. There were moments of frustration, of course. The fire in his eyes would dim as he slammed his fist against the therapy table in defiance. But mostly he exhibited a quiet determination, a flicker of his old self battling its way back.

There was a brief period Jon could be taken from rehab for short car rides, and I would get him out of the building, into the brisk air and watch him enjoy these moments.

The question of Jon's faith had lingered in my mind. Though we weren't a particularly religious family, a sliver of hope prompted me to reach out to our pastor at that time, Pastor Wilson. He agreed, albeit hesitantly, to perform a baptism at the rehab center. It wasn't an elaborate ceremony, but the quiet dignity of the moment resonated deeply. As the pastor spoke the words of baptism, a flicker of recognition crossed Jon's face revealing a sense of peace settling over him. For Dad and me, it was a small act of faith, a way to offer Jon comfort and a connection to something bigger than ourselves.

The day I brought our dachshund, Pooky, to visit Jon, was our last happy moment together. The staff, aware of Jon's deteriorating condition, had relaxed their pet policy. The moment Pooky hopped onto Jon's lap, a spark of joy ignited in his eyes. It was a brief, precious moment, sharing a connection that transcends words. Dad and I sat by his bedside, holding his hand, whispering stories of our childhood, our voices thick with unshed tears. As we said our final goodbyes, a heavy silence filled the room, broken only by the soft snores of Pooky, curled up peacefully beside Jon.

A phone call from Jon's son later that night confirmed our unspoken fears. He was gone. The grief was a physical weight, a suffocating shroud that threatened to consume me. In the days that followed, I found solace in the memories, laughter and tears shared over a lifetime. Jon's absence left a gaping hole in our family, but his spirit and zest for life continues to inspire me. His death also prompted some introspection. The experience with the baptism planted a seed of faith, a belief in something larger than ourselves. It's a seed I continue to nurture, a testament to the enduring love and the profound impact my brother had on my life.

Mom's diagnosis of lung cancer hit us all like a sucker punch. She was a non-smoker who worked in an office thick with second-hand smoke, which had to have had an impact on her lungs. The surgery to remove a portion of her lung was a brutal ordeal, followed by the harsh realities of radiation treatment. Yet, through it all, Mom displayed a quiet strength, a determination to fight for every precious breath. We clung to that strength, to the slivers of hope offered by her doctors. Dad, ever the optimist, saw every positive test result, every doctor's encouraging word, as a victory.

To me, the truth was etched in the deepening lines on her face, the shortness of her breath, the way her vibrant spirit seemed to dim a little each day. It was during one of these visits home that I approached Dad, the unspoken worry hanging heavily in the air. We took a drive, a somber ritual we repeated whenever difficult conversations loomed. "You know her condition is only going to get worse, don't you?" I finally asked, my voice thick with emotion. Dad, his eyes filled with unshed tears, nodded. "I know," he rasped, "but I can't help but hope."

The decision about Jon added another layer of complexity to our already heavy hearts. Jon's condition made traveling long distances a risky proposition. Wouldn't telling him about Mom only add to his suffering? The silence, heavy and unspoken, settled between Dad and me. We decided to spare him the immediate pain, a decision shrouded in both love and guilt.

Dad was no stranger to medical challenges. Even before Mom's illness, his body had endured multiple battles. Double knee replacements, a fall that shattered his hip, and then prostate cancer. He fought through each surgery with grit and determination, a testament to his stubborn will. The radiation treatment to eradicate cancer, however, left an invisible scar. It ravaged his insides, making it a near-constant battle to simply leave the house. The frustration was etched on his face, a simmering anger that sometimes boiled over. But Dad wasn't one to give up easily. He found solace in routine, in the quiet companionship of his Schnauzer dog, Sig. Their daily walks, weather permitting, were a lifeline, a chance to breathe fresh air, to feel the sun on his face, and forget his troubles for a while.

We would go see him occasionally but with us living two hours away and working forty-hour weeks, it was difficult to see how he was actually doing physically and mentally. He took a fall one evening while downtown with friends, messing up his back. An injury that would take considerable time to heal along with proper medication. He called to ask me if I would come get the dog since he was not able to get out to walk him. We drove back to Alta Vista to pick up his dog and returned home the same day.

Dad was on two medications, one for depression and the other for his back pain. We would later find out the two medications taken together could cause an increase in depression. He was home alone, not feeling like going anywhere. We had his faithful K-9 companion. I called him one night around 8 pm to see how he was doing, but he did not sound like himself. He said he was really tired, getting ready for bed. We both said goodbye, then hung up the phone. His cousin also called him that night to talk for a while. According to him he thought he might have gotten Dad out of bed to answer the phone.

While I was at work the following day, a visitor came to my supervisor's office. It was the Fort Leavenworth Army Chaplain from a church on post. He told me Dad had passed away, then asked if there was anything he could do for me. I told him I was okay and he left. Before the chaplain left, he told me to call the county sheriff back home. Thinking this was a bit odd, I made the call.

The sheriff told me the circumstances of Dad's death. He said Dad committed suicide by placing a 22-cal. pistol to his temple and pulling the trigger. I was devastated. The sheriff said the chaplain was supposed to inform me about the cause of death. Dad was eighty-four, so there could be any number of reasons to end his life.

I had no idea Dad was that depressed. He never appeared to be the type of person who would do something like that.

Dad had made the comment several years before he died, he wanted Sig buried with him. If it were not against regulations, I would have had Sig put in the coffin with Dad. Sig may not have been at his side in the coffin, but he is in a vault nearby. Now they are both together for eternity.

Looking back on this journey, I'm struck by the challenges life throws our way, the unexpected turns and the heartbreaking losses. Yet, woven within the fabric of hardship are also moments of immense love, unwavering support, and the enduring strength of the human spirit. These experiences have shaped me, taught me empathy, and instilled in me a deep appreciation for the preciousness of life.

Today, my life is full. I cherish my family and friends, the simple joys of each day. The challenges I faced, the losses I endured. These have all shaped me into the person I am. They've taught me the importance of empathy, resilience, and finding strength in the darkest of times. I hope my story can help someone navigate their own struggles and encourage open conversations about mental health.

If my experiences resonate with anyone out there, I will encourage open conversations about mental health, highlighting the importance of cherishing your loved ones. Let us face life's challenges with courage, embrace the love that surrounds us, and find comfort in the knowledge that even in loss, the bonds we forge leave an everlasting imprint.

If people realize the effects suicide has on loved ones and friends close to them, many might reconsider. It has such a devastating impact. I lost my brother, mom and dad in a three-year period; almost my entire family gone in what seemed to be the flash of an instant.

While I'm not a counselor, and this book is not intended to be a self-help guide, my desire is that it offers hope and an example of someone pushing through his mental and emotional struggles. I rely on my spiritual allegiance and affection of loved ones to help me. I see a psychiatrist on a regular basis to help me through times of depression. Remember there is a vast array of support out there to help anyone who is considering taking their own life. My advice to you is to reach out and ask for help.

ABOUT THE AUTHOR

STEVEN WOELK grew up in Alta Vista, Kansas. At age 18, he joined the US Navy, and served his lone sea duty on the USS Pueblo. On 23 January, 1968, his ship's crew was suddenly and maliciously attacked, seized and taken prisoner by the North Korean Navy. They would spend the next eleven months in captivity, never knowing what horrors would greet them each day. After enduring eleven months of primitive medical treatment, brutal beatings and malnutrition, eighty-two captives were set free at the "Bridge of No Return" on 23 December, 1968. His faith in God, family and country kept him sane throughout his captivity.

This book is about his passion for keeping the legacy and stories of the Pueblo crew alive. He is retired now, but gains strength in fishing, hunting, woodworking, golf, playing country music with his guitar, and sharing coffee breaks with fellow veterans. Steven has been blessed with a forty-eight-year marriage to his wife, Kathy, a son and two wonderful grandchildren.

www.ingramcontent.com/pod-product-compliance
Lightning Source LLC
Chambersburg PA
CBHW051621120626
46551CB00014B/1888